Camping • Fishing • Boating

Bureau
of Reclamation

Lakes Guide

Published by:
Roundabout Publications
P.O. Box 19235 • Lenexa, KS 66285
Phone: 800-455-2207

Please Note

Every effort has been made to make this book as complete and as accurate as possible. However, there may be mistakes both typographical and in content. Therefore, this text should be used as a general guide to the lakes and reservoirs covered. Although we regret any inconvenience caused by inaccurate information, the author and Roundabout Publications shall have neither liability nor responsibility to any person or entity with respect to any loss or damage caused, or alleged to be caused, directly or indirectly by the information contained in this book.

ISBN: 1-885464-02-9

Published by:
Roundabout Publications
P.O. Box 19235 • Lenexa, KS 66285
Phone: 800-455-2207

Contents

Introduction 4

Arizona 7

California 15

Colorado 29

Idaho 44

Kansas 51

Montana 55

Nebraska 60

Nevada 64

New Mexico 68

North Dakota 73

Oklahoma 76

Oregon 79

South Dakota 87

Texas 90

Utah 93

Washington 102

Wyoming 110

Appendix A - Bureau of Reclamation Regions 118

Appendix B - Alphabetical List of Lakes 119

INTRODUCTION

About the Bureau of Reclamation

The Bureau of Reclamation, an agency in the Department of the Interior, provides more than 80 million visitors a year with exciting water-based recreation opportunities at hundreds of reservoirs in 17 western states. Nearly 200 of these recreation areas are managed by non-federal governmental entities, such as state and county parks. Many are managed by other Federal agencies, like the National Park Service and the US Forest Service.

There are over 200 concession operations that offer facilities and services to the public like marinas, campgrounds, swimming beaches, equestrian centers and golf courses. Fishing and boating are the most popular activities, accounting for more than 27 million user days on about 1.7 million surface acres of water. Many of the facilities are accessible to the disabled.

Bureau of Reclamation Lakes Guide

This book is a compilation of the Bureau of Reclamation projects constructed in the western United States. The book lists nearly 250 lakes and reservoirs. The information is provided in a simple to use format that provides basic information about each lake. The project information is divided into three sections as described below.

1) Activities and Facilities Chart

This chart shows at a glance the type of activities and facilities found at each project. Icons are used to represent a particular activity or facility. A bullet (•) in the column beneath the icon indicates that the activity or facility is offered at that lake. A number preceding the row of bullets corresponds to the project number shown on the state map. The icons and what they represent are shown below.

Camping (Includes both developed and primitive.)

Fishing (Also see the *Primary Game Fish* chart.)

Boating (Includes motor boating, sailing, etc.)

Hunting

Trails (Includes hiking, equestrian, off-road, etc.)

Swimming

Picnicking

Marina / Concession Services

Comfort Stations

Visitor and/or Information Center

Handicapped Facilities

2) *Project Location and Recreation Contact*

Following the *Activities and Facilities* chart are the Bureau of Reclamation projects, their location and directions, the agency that manages recreation, and a row of icons further detailing the activities and facilities. A brief description of the icons used in this section is described below.

Primitive Camping

Developed Camping

Hiking Trails

- Bicycling Trails (Paved and other.)
- Equestrian Trails
- Nature Walks / Trails
- Off-Road Vehicle Area / Trails
- Boat Launching Facilities
- Wildlife Viewing
- Disabled Angler Facilities

3) *Primary Game Fish Chart*

Following the *Project Location and Recreation Contact* section is a chart showing the primary species of fish that inhabit each lake.

Abbreviations Used

BLM	Bureau of Land Management
BOR	Bureau of Reclamation
CR	County Road
FSR	Forest Service Road
HMU	Habitat Management Unit
I	Interstate
NF	National Forest
NP	National Park
NRA	National Recreation Area
NWR	National Wildlife Refuge
SH	State Highway
SP	State Park
SRA	State Recreation Area
SWA	State Wildlife Area
US	U.S. Highway
WMA	Wildlife Management Area

ARIZONA

1. Apache Lake
2. Bartlett Reservoir
3. Canyon Lake
4. Cibola NWR
5. Davis Dam - Lake Mohave
6. Lake Havasu
7. Havasu NWR
8. Hoover Dam
9. Horseshoe Reservoir
10. Imperial Reservoir
11. Imperial NWR
12. Lake Mead NRA
13. Lake Pleasant
14. Lake Powell, Glen Canyon NRA
15. Mittry Lake Wildlife Area
16. Saguaro Lake
17. Theodore Roosevelt Lake

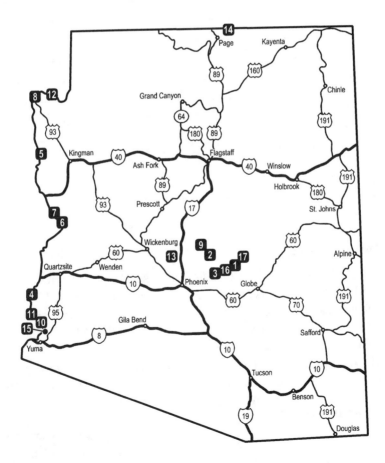

Activities and Facilities

	🏕	🚤	〰	🎣	🚶	🏊	🏓	⚓	🚻	ℹ	♿
1	•	•	•	•	•	•	•	•	•	•	•
2	•	•	•	•	•	•	•	•	•		
3	•	•	•		•	•	•	•	•		
4		•	•	•		•			•	•	
5	•	•	•		•	•	•	•	•	•	•
6	•	•	•		•	•	•	•	•	•	•
7	•	•	•	•	•	•	•	•	•	•	•
8					•				•	•	•
9	•	•	•	•	•	•	•		•	•	
10	•	•	•	•	•	•			•	•	•
11		•	•	•	•		•		•	•	•
12	•	•	•	•	•	•	•	•	•	•	•
13	•	•	•		•	•	•	•	•	•	•
14	•	•	•	•	•	•	•	•	•	•	•
15		•	•	•	•	•	•		•	•	
16	•	•	•		•	•	•	•	•	•	
17	•	•	•	•	•	•	•	•	•	•	

Apache Lake

BOR Region: Lower Colorado. See also Canyon, Saguaro, and Theodore Roosevelt Lakes. Recreation is administered by the U.S. Forest Service and State of Arizona. Located in central Arizona about 65 miles east of Phoenix. From Apachie Junction, follow SH 88 (Apachie Trail) northeast for about 33 miles to the reservoir.

Recreation Contact: Tonto National Forest, 2324 E McDowell Rd., P.O. Box 5348, Phoenix AZ 85010 / 602-225-5200. Arizona Game and Fish Department, Apache Lake, 2221 W Greenway Rd., Phoenix AZ 85023 / 602-942-3000.

Bartlett Reservoir

BOR Region: Lower Colorado. See also Horseshoe Reservoir. Recreation is administered by the U.S. Forest Service and State of Arizona. Located in central Arizona north of Phoenix, 22 miles east of Carefree. From Carefree, follow Cave Creek Road/Horseshoe Dam Road east for about 22 miles.

Recreation Contact: Tonto National Forest, 2324 E McDowell Rd., P.O. Box 5348, Phoenix AZ 85010 / 602-225-5200. Arizona Game and Fish Department, Bartlett Reservoir, 2221 W Greenway Rd., Phoenix AZ 85023 / 602-942-3000.

Canyon Lake

BOR Region: Lower Colorado. See also Apache, Saguaro, and Theodore Roosevelt Lakes. Recreation is administered by the U.S. Forest Service and the State of Arizona. Located in central Arizona about 51 miles east of Phoenix. From Apachie Junction, follow SH 88 (Apachie Trail) northeast 15 miles to the lake.

Recreation Contact: Tonto National Forest, 2324 E McDowell Rd., P.O. Box 5348, Phoenix AZ 85010 / 602-225-5200. Arizona Game and Fish Department, Canyon Lake, 2221 W Greenway Rd., Phoenix AZ 85023 / 602-942-3000.

Cibola National Wildlife Refuge

BOR Region: Lower Colorado. See also Imperial Reservoir and Imperial NWR. Recreation is administered by U.S. Fish and Wildlife Service. Located in southwestern Arizona and southeastern California, 20 miles south of Blythe, California. From Blythe, go approximately 4 miles west on I-10 to Neighbors Boulevard exit. Go south on Neighbors Boulevard for 12 miles to Wayne Sprawls Farmer's Bridge. After crossing the bridge, continue south for 3½ miles to the Cibola NWR Headquarters. The majority of Cibola NWR is located in Arizona, but some areas along the Old River Channel are located in California.

Recreation Contact: U.S. Fish and Wildlife Service, Cibola NWR, Route 2 Box 138, Cibola AZ 85328 / 520-857-3253.

Davis Dam — Lake Mohave

BOR Region: Lower Colorado. See also Hoover Dam and Lake Mead NRA. Recreation is administered by two county agencies and the National Park Service. Located 10 miles north of Bullhead City, on the Arizona side and 8 miles north of Laughlin, on the Nevada side of the Colorado River. From Bullhead City, travel north on SH 95 to Lake Mohave. Lake Mohave is part of the Lake Mead National Recreation Area administered by the National Park Service.

Recreation Contact: Mohave County Parks Department, P.O. Box 390, Kingman AZ 86402 / 602-757-0915. Clark County Parks and Recreation, 304 S 3rd St. Suite 220, Las Vegas NV 89155 / 702-455-8298.

Lake Havasu

BOR Region: Lower Colorado. See also Havasu National Wildlife Refuge. Recreation is administered by the Bureau of Land Management, state and county agencies. Lake Havasu is located in western Arizona and southeast California. The recreation areas are situated between Lake Havasu City, Arizona and Parker, Arizona. The area can be accessed from SH 95, off either I-40 or I-10.

Recreation Contact: U.S. Bureau of Land Management, Lake Havasu Field Office, 2610 Sweetwater Ave., Lake Havasu City AZ 86406 / 520-505-1200. Buckskin Mountains State Park, phone 520-667-3231. Lake Havasu State Park, phone 520-855-2784.

Havasu National Wildlife Refuge

BOR Region: Lower Colorado. See also Lake Havasu. Recreation is administered by the U.S. Fish and Wildlife Service. Located south of I-40 in western Arizona near the California state line, just north of Lake Havasu City off SH 95. To reach the refuge office in Needles, California from I-40, exit on J Street and go southwest to Mesquite Avenue, turn right, follow the signs.

Recreation Contact: U.S. Fish and Wildlife Service, Havasu NWR, P.O. Box 3009, Needles CA 92363 / 760-326-3853.

Hoover Dam

BOR Region: Lower Colorado. See also Lake Mead NRA and Davis Dam—Lake Mohave. Hoover Dam is administered by the Bureau of Reclamation. Located in northwest Arizona and southeast Nevada on US 93. To reach Hoover Dam from Kingman, Arizona travel north on US 93. From Las Vegas, Nevada travel 30 miles southeast on US 93/95.

Recreation Contact: Bureau of Reclamation, Lower Colorado Region, P.O. Box 61470, Boulder City NV 89006 / 702-294-3513.

Horseshoe Reservoir

BOR Region: Lower Colorado. See also Bartlett Reservoir. Recreation is administered by the U.S. Forest Service and State of Arizona. Located in central Arizona, 58 miles northeast of Phoenix. From Carefree, Arizona, follow Cave Creek Road/Horseshoe Dam Road about 12 miles east to Forest Service Road 205. Follow FSR 205 north about 10 miles to the reservoir.

Recreation Contact: Tonto National Forest, 2324 E McDowell Rd., P.O. Box 5348, Phoenix AZ 85010 / 602-225-5200. Arizona Game and Fish Department, Horseshoe Reservoir, 2221 W Greenway Rd., Phoenix AZ 85023 / 602-942-3000.

Imperial Reservoir

BOR Region: Lower Colorado. See also Cibola NWR, Imperial NWR, and Mittry Lake Wildlife Area. Recreation is administered by the Bureau of Land Management and the State of California. Located in southwest Arizona and southeast California, about 30 miles north of Yuma, Arizona. In Arizona the recreation areas are accessed off US 95. In California, Picacho State Park is reached from I-8 Exit 177 near Yuma by following Picacho Road north about 23 miles.

Recreation Contact: U.S. Bureau of Land Management, Lake Havasu Field Office, 2610 Sweetwater Ave., Lake Havasu City AZ 86406 / 520-505-1200. Picacho State Park, P.O. Box 848, Winterhaven CA 92283 / 760-393-3052.

Imperial National Wildlife Refuge

BOR Region: Lower Colorado. See also Cibola NWR, Imperial Reservoir and Mittry Lake Wildlife Area. Recreation is administered by the U.S. Fish and Wildlife Service. Located in southwest Arizona about 38 miles north of Yuma off US 95. From Yuma, go north on US 95 for 25 miles to Martinez Lake Road. Turn west and travel 13 miles; follow signs to visitor center.

Recreation Contact: U.S. Fish and Wildlife Service, Imperial NWR, P.O. Box 72217, Yuma AZ 85365 / 520-783-3371.

Lake Mead National Recreation Area

BOR Region: Lower Colorado. See also Davis Dam—Lake Mohave and Hoover Dam. The National Park Service manages all the resources within the NRA boundaries. Located in northwestern Arizona and southeast Nevada. This large area can be accessed from several points off I-15 in Nevada and from US 93 in Arizona, north of Kingman. Lake Mead Visitor Center is located on Nevada SH 166 (Lakeshore Road) just off US 93. Katherine Ranger Station on Lake Mohave is located on the Katherine Access Road off Arizona SH 68 by Davis Dam. The area includes Lake Mead, located 30 miles southeast of Las Vegas, and Lake Mohave, downstream from Hoover Dam.

Recreation Contact: National Park Service, Lake Mead NRA, 601 Nevada Hwy., Boulder City NV 89005 / 702-293-8990.

Lake Pleasant

BOR Region: Lower Colorado. The recreation at Lake Pleasant is administered by county and state agencies. Located in central Arizona approximately 35 miles northwest of Phoenix. The reservoir can be accessed off SH 74, east of Morristown.

Recreation Contact: Maricopa County Parks and Recreation Department, 3475 W Durango, Phoenix AZ 85009 / 602-506-2903. Arizona Game and Fish Department, Lake Pleasant, 2221 W Greenway Rd., Phoenix AZ 85023 / 602-942-3000.

Lake Powell — Glen Canyon NRA

BOR Region: Upper Colorado. Recreation is administered by the National Park Service. Located in northern Arizona and southern Utah, just outside of Page, Arizona. Access is off US 89 from either state.

Recreation Contact: National Park Service, Glen Canyon NRA, P.O. Box 1507, Page AZ 86040 / 520-608-6404 general information, 520-608-6200 headquarters.

Mittry Lake Wildlife Area

BOR Region: Lower Colorado. Also see Imperial Reservoir and Imperial NWR. Recreation is administered by the State of Arizona. Located in southwest Arizona about 20 miles northeast of Yuma. The area can be accessed off US 95.

Recreation Contact: Arizona Game and Fish Department, Mittry Lake Wildlife Area, 9140 E County 10½ St., Yuma AZ 85365 / 520-342-0091.

Saguaro Lake

BOR Region: Lower Colorado. See also Apache, Canyon, and Theodore Roosevelt Lakes. Recreation is administered by the Bureau of Reclamation and State of Arizona. Located 41 miles northeast of Phoenix in central Arizona. Take the Bush Highway north from US 60 to the Saguaro del Norte Recreation Site turnoff. You can also take the Beeline Highway (SH 87) from either the McDowell Road turnoff in Mesa or from Shea Boulevard near Fountain Hills. About 8 miles after crossing the Verde River, turn right at signs indicating the Saguaro Lake Recreation Area.

Recreation Contact: Bureau of Reclamation, Phoenix Area Office, 2222 W Dunlap Ave., Suite 100, Phoenix AZ 85021 / 602-216-3999. Arizona Game and Fish Department, Saguaro Lake, 2221 W Greenway Rd., Phoenix AZ 85023 / 602-942-3000.

Theodore Roosevelt Lake

BOR Region: Lower Colorado. See also Apache, Canyon, and Saguaro Lakes. Recreation is administered by the U.S. Forest Service. Located

76 miles northeast of Phoenix and 30 miles northwest of Globe. From Apachie Junction take the Apachie Trail (SH 88) northeast to the reservoir. From Globe follow SH 88 northwest off US 60.

Recreation Contact: Tonto National Forest, 2324 E McDowell Rd., P.O. Box 5348, Phoenix AZ 85010 / 602-225-5200.

Primary Game Fish

	Bass	Bluegill	Catfish	Crappie	Pike	Perch	Salmon	Trout	Walleye
1 Apache Lake	•	•	•	•					•
2 Bartlett Reservoir	•	•	•	•					
3 Canyon Lake	•	•	•	•				•	•
4 Cibola NWR	•	•	•	•		•			
5 Davis Dam - Lake Mohave	•		•					•	
6 Lake Havasu	•	•	•	•					
7 Havasu NWR	•		•						
8 Hoover Dam									
9 Horseshoe Reservoir	•		•	•					
10 Imperial Reservoir	•		•						
11 Imperial NWR	•	•	•	•					
12 Lake Mead NRA	•	•	•	•				•	
13 Lake Pleasant	•		•	•					
14 Lake Powell, Glen Canyon NRA	•		•	•	•			•	•
15 Mittry Lake Wildlife Area	•	•	•	•			•		
16 Saguaro Lake	•	•	•	•				•	•
17 Theodore Roosevelt Lake	•	•	•	•			•	•	

CALIFORNIA

1 Boca Reservoir
2 Cachuma Lake
3 Cibola NWR
4 Contra Loma Reservoir
5 East Park Reservoir
6 Folsom Lake
7 Lake Havasu
8 Havasu NWR
9 Imperial Reservoir

10 Imperial NWR
11 Jenkinson Lake
12 Keswick Reservoir
13 Lake Berryessa
14 Lake Cahuilla
15 Lake Casitas
16 Lake Solano
17 Lake Tahoe
18 Lake Woollomes
19 Lewiston Lake
20 Little Panoche Dam
21 Los Banos Reservoir
22 Millerton Lake
23 Mittry Lake Wildlife Area
24 New Melones Lake
25 Prosser Creek Reservoir
26 Salton Sea SRA & NWR
27 San Justo Reservoir
28 San Luis Reservoir
29 Shasta Lake
30 Squaw Leap Mgmt. Area

31 Stampede Reservoir
32 Stony Gorge Reservoir
33 Sugar Pine Reservoir
34 Trinity Lake
35 Whiskeytown Lake

Activities and Facilities

#	Camping	Boating	Boat Ramp	Fishing	Hiking	Swimming	Picnic	Marina/Anchorage	Restrooms	Information	Accessible
1	•	•	•	•	•	•	•		•		•
2	•	•	•		•	•	•	•	•	•	•
3		•	•	•		•			•	•	
4		•	•		•	•	•	•	•	•	•
5	•	•	•		•	•	•		•		
6	•	•	•		•	•	•	•	•	•	•
7	•	•	•		•	•	•	•	•	•	•
8	•	•	•	•	•	•	•	•	•	•	•
9	•	•	•	•	•	•			•	•	•
10		•	•	•	•		•		•	•	•
11	•	•	•		•	•	•		•		
12	•	•	•	•	•	•	•	•	•		•
13	•	•	•		•	•	•	•	•	•	
14	•	•	•		•	•	•	•	•	•	•
15	•	•	•		•		•	•	•	•	•
16	•	•	•		•	•	•		•		
17	•	•	•		•	•	•	•	•	•	•
18		•	•		•	•	•		•		
19	•	•	•	•	•	•	•	•	•	•	•
20		•		•			•		•		
21	•	•	•	•	•	•	•		•		
22	•	•	•	•	•	•	•	•	•	•	
23		•	•	•	•	•	•		•	•	
24	•	•	•	•	•	•	•	•	•	•	•
25	•	•	•	•	•	•	•		•		
26	•	•	•	•	•	•	•	•	•	•	•
27		•	•		•		•		•	•	
28	•	•	•	•	•	•	•		•		•
29	•	•	•	•	•	•	•	•	•	•	•
30	•	•			•		•		•	•	•

Activities and Facilities *(continued)*

	⛺	🦆	〰️	🎣	🚶	🏊	⛽	⚓	🚻	*i*	♿
31	•	•	•	•	•	•	•		•		•
32	•	•	•		•	•	•		•		•
33	•	•	•		•	•	•		•		
34	•	•	•	•	•	•	•	•	•	•	•
35	•	•	•	•	•	•	•	•	•	•	•

Boca Reservoir

BOR Region: Mid-Pacific. See also Stampede and Prosser Creek Reservoirs. Recreation managed by the U.S. Forest Service. Located north of Lake Tahoe in northeast California, one mile north of I-80 near Truckee.

Recreation Contact: Tahoe National Forest, Truckee Ranger District, 10342 Hwy. 89 N, Truckee CA 96161 / 530-587-3558.

Cachuma Lake

BOR Region: Mid-Pacific. Recreation is administered by Santa Barbara County. Located in southwestern California northwest of Santa Barbara. The reservoir can be accessed off SH 154, south of Santa Ynez.

Recreation Contact: Santa Barbara County Parks Department, 610 Mission Canyon Road, Santa Barbara CA 93105 / 805-568-2461.

Cibola National Wildlife Refuge

BOR Region: Lower Colorado. See also Imperial Reservoir and Imperial NWR. Recreation is administered by U.S. Fish and Wildlife Service. Located in southwestern Arizona and southeastern California, 20 miles south of Blythe, California. From Blythe, go approximately 4 miles west on I-10 to Neighbors Boulevard exit. Go south on Neighbors

Boulevard for 12 miles to Wayne Sprawls Farmer's Bridge. After crossing the bridge, continue south for 3½ miles to the Cibola NWR Headquarters. The majority of Cibola NWR is located in Arizona, but some areas along the Old River Channel are located in California.

Recreation Contact: U.S. Fish and Wildlife Service, Cibola NWR, Route 2 Box 138, Cibola AZ 85328 / 520-857-3253.

Contra Loma Reservoir

BOR Region: Mid-Pacific. Recreation is administered by East Bay Regional Park District. Contra Loma Reservoir is in western California, east of San Francisco. The area is accessible from SH 4, one mile south of the community of Antioch.

Recreation Contact: East Bay Regional Park District, 1200 Frederickson Ln., Antioch CA 94509 / 925-757-2620.

East Park Reservoir

BOR Region: Mid-Pacific. See also Stony Gorge Reservoir. Recreation is administered by the Bureau of Reclamation. Located in north-central California, west of I-5, 23 miles northwest of Maxwell in Colusa County. The reservoir can be reached by traveling west on Maxwell-Sites Road about 9 miles, then west for 14 miles on Sites-Lodoga Road.

Recreation Contact: Bureau of Reclamation, 16349 Shasta Dam Blvd., Shasta Lake CA 96019 / 530-257-1554.

Folsom Lake

BOR Region: Mid-Pacific. Recreation managed by California Department of Parks and Recreation. Folsom Lake is located 20 miles northeast of Sacramento. The lake can be reached from I-80 Exit 109 near Roseville by traveling 5 miles east on Douglas Boulevard. It can also be reached from US 50 by traveling north on Prairie City Road to Folsom, then north on Folsom-Auburn Road.

Recreation Contact: Folsom Lake State Recreation Area, 7806 Folsom Auburn Rd., Folsom CA 95630 / 916-988-0205.

Lake Havasu

BOR Region: Lower Colorado. See also Havasu National Wildlife Refuge. Recreation is administered by the Bureau of Land Management, state and county agencies. Lake Havasu is located in western Arizona and southeast California. The recreation areas are situated between Lake Havasu City, Arizona and Parker, Arizona. The area can be accessed from SH 95, off either I-40 or I-10.

Recreation Contact: U.S. Bureau of Land Management, Lake Havasu Field Office, 2610 Sweetwater Ave., Lake Havasu City AZ 86406 / 520-505-1200. Buckskin Mountains State Park, phone 520-667-3231. Lake Havasu State Park, phone 520-855-2784.

Havasu National Wildlife Refuge

BOR Region: Lower Colorado. See also Lake Havasu. Recreation is administered by the U.S. Fish and Wildlife Service. Located south of I-40 in western Arizona near the California state line, just north of Lake Havasu City off SH 95. To reach the refuge office in Needles, California from I-40, exit on J Street and go southwest to Mesquite Avenue, turn right, follow the signs.

Recreation Contact: U.S. Fish and Wildlife Service, Havasu NWR, P.O. Box 3009, Needles CA 92363 / 760-326-3853.

Imperial Reservoir

BOR Region: Lower Colorado. See also Cibola NWR, Imperial NWR, and Mittry Lake Wildlife Area. Recreation is administered by the Bureau of Land Management and the State of California. Located in southwest Arizona and southeast California, about 30 miles north of Yuma, Arizona. In Arizona the recreation areas are accessed off US 95. In California, Picacho State Park is reached from I-8 Exit 177 near Yuma by following Picacho Road north about 23 miles.

Recreation Contact: U.S. Bureau of Land Management, Lake Havasu Field Office, 2610 Sweetwater Ave., Lake Havasu City AZ 86406 / 520-505-1200. Picacho State Park, P.O. Box 848, Winterhaven CA 92283 / 760-393-3052.

Imperial National Wildlife Refuge

BOR Region: Lower Colorado. See also Cibola NWR, Imperial Reservoir and Mittry Lake Wildlife Area. Recreation is administered by the U.S. Fish and Wildlife Service. Located in southwest Arizona about 38 miles north of Yuma off US 95. From Yuma, go north on US 95 for 25 miles to Martinez Lake Road. Turn west and travel 13 miles; follow signs to visitor center.

Recreation Contact: U.S. Fish and Wildlife Service, Imperial NWR, P.O. Box 72217, Yuma AZ 85365 / 520-783-3371.

Jenkinson Lake

BOR Region: Mid-Pacific. Recreation is administered by the El Dorado Irrigation District. Located in northeastern California, east of Sacramento. The lake is reached from US 50 near Pollock Pines by following CR E16 (Sly Park Road) south about 4 miles.

Recreation Contact: Sly Park Recreation Area, Sly Park Rd., Pollock Pines CA 95726 / 530-644-2545.

Keswick Reservoir

BOR Region: Mid-Pacific. See also Shasta and Whiskeytown Lakes. Recreation is administered by Shasta County. Located in northern California 4 miles northwest of Redding. The reservoir is accessed from SH 299.

Recreation Contact: Shasta County, 1855 Placer, Redding CA 96001 / 530-225-5661.

Lake Berryessa

BOR Region: Mid-Pacific. See also Lake Solano. Recreation is administered by the Bureau of Reclamation. Located in northern California north of San Francisco and west of Sacramento. The lake can be reached from Winters off I-505 by traveling west on SH 128.

Recreation Contact: Bureau of Reclamation, Lake Berryessa Recreation Office, P.O. Box 9332, Spanish Flat Station, Napa CA 94558 / 707-966-2111.

Lake Cahuilla

BOR Region: Lower Colorado. See also Salton Sea SRA & NWA. Recreation is administered by Riverside County. Located in southern California, southeast of Palm Springs. From Indio, travel west on SH 111 to Jefferson Street and follow Jefferson Street south about 5 miles to lake.

Recreation Contact: County of Riverside Parks and Recreation, Lake Cahuilla County Park, 58075 Jefferson St., La Quinta CA 92253 / 760-564-4712.

Lake Casitas

BOR Region: Mid-Pacific. Recreation is administered by Casitas Municipal Water District. Lake Casitas is located about 13 miles north of Ventura near the Los Padres National Forest. To reach the lake from Ojai, follow SH 150 west about 8 miles.

Recreation Contact: Casitas Municipal Water District, 11311 Santa Ana Rd., Ventura CA 93001 / 805-649-2233 information, 805-649-1122 reservations.

Lake Solano

BOR Region: Mid-Pacific. See also Lake Berryessa. Recreation is administered by the County. Located in northern California north of San Francisco and west of Sacramento. To reach the lake from I-505 near Winters, travel west on SH 128 and Pleasants Valley Rd.

Recreation Contact: Lake Solano County Park, 8685 Pleasants Valley Rd., Winters CA 95664 / 530-795-2990.

Lake Tahoe

BOR Region: Mid-Pacific. Recreation is administered by the U.S. Forest Service, State of California and Nevada. Located in eastern California and western Nevada. The Lake can be accessed from SH 89, off I-80 just west of Truckee, California. The Taylor Creek Visitor Center offers a wide range of maps, brochures, wilderness permits, and interpretive programs about the area. The visitor center is located near Fallen Leaf Lake, in South Lake Tahoe, California off SH 89.

Recreation Contact: Lake Tahoe Basin Management Unit, 870 Emerald Bay Road Suite 1, South Lake Tahoe CA 96150 / 530-583-4379. Lake Tahoe Nevada State Park, 2005 Hwy 28, Incline Village NV 89452 / 702-831-0494. Emerald Bay State Park, State Route 89, Tahoe City CA 96142 / 530-525-7277. D.L. Bliss State Park, P.O. Box 266, Tahoma CA 96142 / 530-525-7232.

Lake Woollomes

BOR Region: Mid-Pacific. Recreation is administered by Kern County. Lake Woollomes is located about 30 miles north of Bakersfield in central California, 3 miles southeast of Delano. Easy access from the north or southbound lanes of SH 99. Follow the Pond Road/Lake Woollomes Exit east to the lake.

Recreation Contact: Kern County Parks and Recreation Dept., 1110 Golden State Ave., Bakersfield CA 93301 / 805-868-7000.

Lewiston Lake

BOR Region: Mid-Pacific. See also Trinity and Whiskeytown Lakes. Recreation is administered by the U.S. Forest Service. Located in northern California, northeast of Redding. From Redding travel west on SH 299 to Trinity Dam Blvd, then north to lake. Lewiston Lake is part of the Whiskeytown-Shasta-Trinity NRA.

Recreation Contact: Trinity National Forest, Weaverville Ranger District, P.O. Box 1190, Weaverville CA 96093 / 530-623-2121.

Little Panoche Dam

BOR Region: Mid-Pacific. See also Los Banos and San Luis Reservoirs. Recreation is administered by the State of California. Located in west-central California, about 18 miles south of Los Banos. To reach the dam from I-5 Exit 379, follow CR J1 (Little Panoche Road) west about 5 miles. The lake is on the south side of the road.

Recreation Contact: California Department of Fish and Game, Little Panoche Dam, 18110 W Henry Miller Ave., Los Banos CA 93635 / 209-826-0463.

Los Banos Reservoir

BOR Region: Mid-Pacific. See also Little Panoche Dam and San Luis Reservoir. Recreation is administered by the State of California. Los Banos Reservoir lies about 6 miles southwest of the community of Las Banos, in west-central California. It can be reached from Los Banos by following Pioneer Road west approximately 3 miles to Canyon Road. Follow Canyon Road south to the reservoir.

Recreation Contact: California Dept. of Parks and Recreation, Los Banos Reservoir, 31426 Gustine Rd., Gustine CA 95322 / 209-826-1198.

Millerton Lake

BOR Region: Mid-Pacific. See also Squaw Leap Management Area. Recreation is administered by the State of California. Located in central California, about 20 miles northeast of Fresno. The Lake can be accessed off SH 41 by traveling east on Friant Road.

Recreation Contact: Millerton Lake State Recreation Area, 5290 Millerton Rd., P.O. Box 205, Friant CA 93626 / 559-822-2225.

Mittry Lake Wildlife Area

BOR Region: Lower Colorado. Also see Imperial Reservoir and Imperial NWR. Recreation is administered by the State of Arizona. Located in southwest Arizona about 20 miles northeast of Yuma. The area can be accessed off US 95.

Recreation Contact: Arizona Game and Fish Department, Mittry Lake Wildlife Area, 9140 E County 10½ St., Yuma AZ 85365 / 520-342-0091.

New Melones Lake

BOR Region: Mid-Pacific. Recreation is administered by the Bureau of Reclamation. Located in north-central California, northeast of Modesto. To reach the lake from Sonora, travel northwest on SH 49.

Recreation Contact: Bureau of Reclamation, New Melones Office, 6850 Studhorse Flat Rd., Sonora CA 95370 / 209-536-9094.

Prosser Creek Reservoir

BOR Region: Mid-Pacific. See also Boca and Stampede Reservoirs. Recreation provided by the U.S. Forest Service. Located north of Lake Tahoe and I-80 in northeast California, 3 miles east of SH 89, north of Truckee.

Recreation Contact: Tahoe National Forest, Truckee Ranger District, 10342 Hwy 89 N, Truckee CA 96161 / 530-587-3558.

Salton Sea SRA and NWR

BOR Region: Lower Colorado. See also Lake Cahuilla. Recreation is administered by the State of California and U.S. Fish and Wildlife Service. Located in southern California, southeast of Palm Springs. The east side of the area can be reached off I-10 by traveling south on SH 111. The west side is reached from SH 86 south, off I-10.

Recreation Contact: Salton Sea SRA, 100-225 State Park Road, Northshore CA 92254 / 760-393-3052. U.S. Fish and Wildlife Service, Salton Sea NWR, 906 West Sinclair Rd., Calipatria CA 92233 / 760-348-5278.

San Justo Reservoir

BOR Region: Mid-Pacific. Recreation is administered by San Benito County. Located in western California, south of San Jose, near Hollister. To reach the reservoir from Hollister, follow SH 156 west for about 3 miles to Union Road. Follow Union Road south to the lake.

Recreation Contact: San Benito County, San Justo Reservoir, 2265 Union Rd., Hollister CA 95023 / 831-638-3300.

San Luis Reservoir

BOR Region: Mid-Pacific. See also Little Panoche Dam and Los Banos Reservoir. Recreation administered by the State of California. Located in west-central California approximately 15 miles west of Los Banos on SH 152. Recreation areas include O'Neill Forebay, San Luis Reservoir, and Los Banos Reservoir. All are part of the California Water Project.

Recreation Contact: California Department of Parks and Recreation, San Luis Reservoir SRA, 31426 W Hwy 152, Santa Nella CA 95322 / 209-826-1196.

Shasta Lake

BOR Region: Mid-Pacific. See also Whiskeytown Lake and Keswick Reservoir. Recreation is administered by the U.S. Forest Service. Located in northern California, 12 miles north of Redding. Several access points are available off I-5. The lake is part of the Whiskeytown-Shasta-Trinity NRA.

Recreation Contact: Shasta National Forest, 14225 Holiday Rd., Redding CA 96003 / 530-275-1587.

Squaw Leap Management Area

BOR Region: Mid-Pacific. See also Millerton Lake. Recreation is administered by the Bureau of Land Management. Located in central California about 20 miles northeast of Fresno and 5 miles northwest of Auberry. Located in the upper reaches of Millerton Lake, the area can be reached from the town of Auberry, which is located north of SH 168.

Recreation Contact: Bureau of Land Management, Folsum Field Office, 63 Natoma St., Folsum CA 95630 / 916-985-4474.

Stampede Reservoir

BOR Region: Mid-Pacific. See also Boca and Prosser Creek Reservoirs. Recreation administered by the U.S. Forest Service. Located north of Lake Tahoe in northeastern California. The reservoir is accessed 7 miles north of I-80 near Truckee, off SH 89.

Recreation Contact: Tahoe National Forest, Truckee Ranger District, 10342 Hwy. 89 N., Truckee CA 96161 / 530-587-3558.

Stony Gorge Reservoir

BOR Region: Mid-Pacific. See also East Park Reservoir. Recreation is administered by the Bureau of Reclamation. Located in north-central

California west of I-5, 21 miles west of Willows. The reservoir can be reached off SH 162 and Maxwell Stony Gorge Road.

Recreation Contact: Bureau of Reclamation, 16349 Shasta Dam Blvd., Shasta Lake CA 96019 / 530-257-1554.

Sugar Pine Reservoir

BOR Region: Mid-Pacific. Recreation administered by the U.S. Forest service. Located in northeastern California, west of Lake Tahoe. From Foresthill travel 7 miles northeast on Foresthill Divide Road, then about 9 miles west on Forest Service Road 10.

Recreation Contact: Tahoe National Forest, Foresthill Ranger District, Foresthill Divide Rd., Foresthill CA 95631 / 530-367-2224.

Trinity Lake

BOR Region: Mid-Pacific. See also Lewiston and Whiskeytown Lakes. Recreation is administered by the U.S. Forest Service. Located in northern California, northwest of Redding. From Redding travel west on SH 299 to Weaverville, then north on SH 3. Trinity Lake (also known as Clair Engle) is part of the Whiskeytown-Shasta-Trinity NRA.

Recreation Contact: Trinity National Forest, Weaverville Ranger District, P.O. Box 1190, Weaverville CA 96093 / 530-623-2121.

Whiskeytown Lake

BOR Region: Mid-Pacific. See also Keswick Reservoir and Lewiston Lake. Recreation is administered by the National Park Service. Located in northern California, approximately 8 miles west of Redding. Access to the lake is from SH 299. Of the three parts of the Whiskeytown-Shasta-Trinity NRA, the Whiskeytown Unit is the only unit administered by the National Park Service.

Recreation Contact: National Park Service, Whiskeytown NRA, P.O. Box 188, Whiskeytown CA 96095 / 530-241-6584 headquarters, 530-246-1225 visitor center.

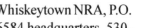

Primary Game Fish

	Bass	Bluegill	Catfish	Crappie	Pike	Perch	Salmon	Trout	Walleye
1 Boca Reservoir								•	•
2 Cachuma Lake	•	•	•	•		•		•	
3 Cibola NWR	•	•	•	•		•			
4 Contra Loma Reservoir	•	•	•	•				•	
5 East Park Reservoir	•	•	•	•					
6 Folsom Lake	•	•	•	•		•		•	
7 Lake Havasu	•	•	•	•					
8 Havasu NWR	•		•						
9 Imperial Reservoir	•		•						
10 Imperial NWR	•	•	•	•					
11 Jenkinson Lake	•	•	•	•				•	
12 Keswick Reservoir								•	
13 Lake Berryessa	•	•	•	•				•	
14 Lake Cahuilla	•		•					•	
15 Lake Casitas	•	•	•	•			•	•	
16 Lake Solano	•	•	•	•				•	
17 Lake Tahoe								•	•
18 Lake Woollomes	•			•	•				
19 Lewiston Lake								•	
20 Little Panoche Dam	•	•	•						
21 Los Banos Reservoir	•	•	•	•				•	
22 Millerton Lake	•	•	•	•				•	
23 Mittry Lake Wildlife Area	•	•	•	•			•		
24 New Melones Lake	•	•	•	•				•	
25 Prosser Creek Reservoir								•	
26 Salton Sea SRA and NWR	Corvina, Tilapia, Croaker, Sargo, Mullet								
27 San Justo Reservoir	•	•	•	•				•	
28 San Luis Reservoir	•	•	•	•				•	
29 Shasta Lake	•	•	•	•			•	•	

Primary Game Fish *(continued)*

	Bass	Bluegill	Catfish	Crappie	Pike	Perch	Salmon	Trout	Walleye
30 Squaw Leap Mgmt. Area	•	•	•	•				•	
31 Stampede Reservoir								•	•
32 Stony Gorge Reservoir	•	•	•	•					
33 Sugar Pine Reservoir	•	•						•	
34 Trinity Lake	•		•					•	•
35 Whiskeytown Lake	•	•	•					•	•

COLORADO

1 Blue Mesa Reservoir
2 Bonham Reservoir
3 Bonny Reservoir
4 Carter Lake
5 Colorado River WA
6 Cottonwood #1 Reservoir
7 Crawford Reservoir
8 Crystal Reservoir
9 East Portal Reservoir
10 Flatiron Reservoir
11 Fruitgrowers Reservoir
12 Green Mountain Camp
13 Green Mountain Reservoir
14 Gunnison River
15 Horsethief Canyon SWA
16 Horsetooth Reservoir
17 Jackson Gulch Reservoir
18 Lake Estes
19 Lake Granby
20 Lemon Reservoir
21 Marys Lake
22 McPhee Reservoir
23 Morrow Point Reservoir
24 Navajo Reservoir
25 Paonia Reservoir
26 Pinewood Lake
27 Platoro Reservoir
28 Pueblo Reservoir
29 Ridgway Reservoir
30 Rifle Gap Reservoir
31 Ruedi Reservoir
32 Shadow Mountain Lake
33 Silver Jack Reservoir
34 Taylor Park Reservoir
35 Taylor River SWA
36 Turquoise Lake
37 Twin Lakes Reservoir
38 Vallecito Reservoir
39 Vega Reservoir
40 Willow Creek Reservoir

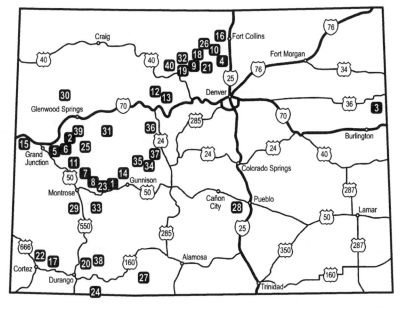

Activities and Facilities

#	Camping	Boating	Water Sports	Fishing	Hiking	Swimming	Picnic	Marina	Restrooms	Information	Accessible
1	•	•	•	•	•	•	•	•		•	•
2		•									
3	•	•	•	•	•	•	•	•	•	•	•
4	•	•	•		•	•	•	•	•		
5		•	•		•				•		•
6	•	•	•		•						
7	•	•	•	•	•	•	•		•	•	•
8	•	•	•	•	•		•				
9	•	•			•		•		•		
10	•	•					•		•		
11		•	•	•	•						•
12		•			•		•				
13	•	•	•	•	•	•	•	•	•		
14		•									
15		•	•	•	•						
16	•	•	•		•	•	•	•	•	•	
17	•	•	•	•	•		•		•	•	
18		•	•		•	•	•	•	•	•	•
19	•	•	•	•	•	•	•	•	•	•	•
20	•	•	•	•	•		•		•	•	
21	•	•			•	•	•		•		
22	•	•	•	•	•		•	•	•	•	•
23	•	•	•	•	•		•	•	•	•	
24	•	•	•	•	•	•	•	•	•	•	•
25	•	•	•	•			•		•		
26	•	•	•		•	•	•		•		
27	•	•	•	•	•		•		•		
28	•	•	•	•	•	•	•	•	•	•	•
29	•	•	•	•	•	•	•	•	•	•	•
30	•	•	•	•		•	•		•		

Activities and Facilities *(continued)*

	⛺	🦆	🛟	🎣	🚶	🏊	⛱	⚓	🚻	ℹ️	♿
31	•	•	•	•	•	•	•		•		
32	•	•	•	•	•	•	•	•	•		
33	•	•	•	•	•		•		•		
34	•	•	•	•	•		•		•		
35		•									
36	•	•	•		•		•		•		
37	•	•	•	•	•		•		•	•	•
38	•	•	•	•	•		•	•	•	•	
39	•	•	•	•	•		•		•	•	
40	•	•	•	•	•	•	•		•		

Blue Mesa Reservoir

BOR Region: Upper Colorado. See also Crawford, Crystal, Morrow Point and Silver Jack Reservoirs. Recreation is administered by the National Park Service. Located in west-central Colorado, west of Gunnison. From Gunnison go about 18 miles west on US 50 to the recreation area entrance. Blue Mesa Reservoir is one of three reservoirs included as part of the Curecanti National Recreation Area.

Recreation Contact: National Park Service, Curecanti National Recreation Area, 102 Elk Creek, Gunnison CO 81230 / 970-641-2337.

Bonham Reservoir

BOR Region: Upper Colorado. See also Cottonwood #1 and Vega Reservoirs. Recreation is administered by the U.S. Forest Service. Located in western Colorado east of Grand Junction. From the junction with I-70, travel west about 22 miles on SH 65 and 330 to Collbran. From Collbran head south about 13 miles on Bonham Road and Forest Service Road 121 to the reservoir (follow signs from Collbran).

Recreation Contact: Grand Mesa National Forest, Grand Junction Ranger District, 764 Horizon Dr., Grand Junction CO 81506 / 970-242-8211.

Bonny Reservoir

BOR Region: Great Plains. Recreation is administered by the State of Colorado. Located in eastern Colorado, 25 miles north of Burlington. Follow US 385, 23 miles north to either County Road 2 or 3 east.

Recreation Contact: Bonny Lake State Park, 30010 CR 3 Box 78A, Idalia CO 80735 / 970-354-7306.

Carter Lake

BOR Region: Great Plains. See also Flatiron Reservoir and Pinewood Lake. Recreation is administered by Larimer County. Located in north central Colorado, southwest of Ft. Collins near Loveland. To reach the lake from Loveland, follow US 34 west about 7 miles to CR 29. Follow CR 29 south 2 miles to CR 18E and turn west. Follow CR 18E about 2 miles to CR 31 and turn south. Follow CR 31 south to the lake.

Recreation Contact: Larimer County Parks Department, Carter Lake, 1800 S County Road 31, Loveland CO 80537 / 970-679-4570.

Colorado River Wildlife Area

BOR Region: Upper Colorado. See also Horsethief Canyon State Wildlife Area. Recreation is administered by the State of Colorado. Located in western Colorado, south of Grand Junction. From the junction of US 50 and SH 141 in Whitewater, travel north on SH 141 (32 Road) to D Road, then 2 miles west to 30 Road, then south to property.

Recreation Contact: Colorado River State Park, 375 32 Rd., Clifton CO 81520 / 970-434-3388.

Cottonwood #1 Reservoir

BOR Region: Upper Colorado. See also Bonham and Vega Reservoirs. Recreation is administered by the U.S. Forest Service. Located in western Colorado east of Grand Junction. From the junction with I-70, travel west about 22 miles on SH 65 and 330 to Collbran. From Collbran head south about 14 miles on Bonham Road and Forest Service Road 121 to the junction with Forest Service Road 257, then west about 5 miles to the reservoir. Portions of the road leading to the reservoir are very rough, use caution.

Recreation Contact: Grand Mesa National Forest, Grand Junction Ranger District, 764 Horizon Dr., Grand Junction CO 81506 / 970-242-8211.

Crawford Reservoir

BOR Region: Upper Colorado. See also Blue Mesa, Crystal, and Morrow Point Reservoirs. Recreation is administered by the State of Colorado. Located in western Colorado, east of Delta. From Delta travel east on SH 92 to Hotchkiss, then south on SH 92 to Crawford. The park entrance is one mile south of Crawford off SH 92.

Recreation Contact: Crawford State Park, P.O. Box 147, Crawford CO 81415 / 970-921-5721.

Crystal Reservoir

BOR Region: Upper Colorado. See also Blue Mesa, Crawford, and Morrow Point Reservoirs. Recreation is administered by the National Park Service. No road access to the reservoir; access by foot trail or boat only. Mesa Creek Trail (1.5 miles, easy to moderately strenuous) is located off US 50, 1 mile north of Cimarron via Cimarron Dr. Boating access via the Gunnison River from below Morrow Point Dam. Boating limited to hand-carried craft. To reach the Gunnison River below Crystal Dam go about 8 miles east from Montrose on US 50 to SH 347, then approximately 6 miles north to the East Portal Rd., and approximately 4 miles to the river. Note: About 2 miles of this access is a very steep winding road; no motorhomes or trailers allowed. Road closed to all vehicles from about October 15 to about May 15, depending on weather. Crystal Reservoir is one of three reservoirs included as part of the Curecanti National Recreation Area.

Recreation Contact: National Park Service, Curecanti NRA, 102 Elk Creek, Gunnison CO 81230 / 970-641-2337.

East Portal Reservoir

BOR Region: Great Plains. See also Lake Estes and Mary's Lake. Recreation is administered by the Estes Valley Recreation and Park District. Located in northern Colorado near the Rocky Mountain NP. To reach the area from Estes Park, follow US 36 west to SH 66, then south to Tunnel Road and turn west. Follow Tunnel Road to the reservoir.

Recreation Contact: Estes Valley Recreation and Park District, P.O. Box 1379, Estes Park CO 80517 / 970-586-8191.

Flatiron Reservoir

BOR Region: Great Plains. See also Carter and Pinewood Lakes. Recreation is administered by Larimer County. Located in northern Colorado near Loveland. From Loveland, follow US 36 west about 7 miles to CR 29. Follow CR 29 south 2 miles to CR 18E and turn west. Follow CR 18E to the reservoir.

Recreation Contact: Larimer County Parks Department, Flatiron Reservoir, 1800 S County Road 31, Loveland CO 80537 / 970-679-4570.

Fruitgrowers Reservoir

BOR Region: Upper Colorado. Recreation is administered by the Bureau of Reclamation. Located in western Colorado southeast of Grand Junction. From the junction of US 50 and SH 92 at Delta, travel east about 4 miles on SH 92 to SH 65, then north on SH 65 about 5 miles to Road 2100, turn right for approximately 100 yards to Road M (Antelope Hill Sign), turn left and travel about one mile to the reservoir.

Recreation Contact: Bureau of Reclamation, 2764 Compass Dr., Grand Junction CO 81506 / 970-248-0617.

Green Mountain Camp

BOR Region: Great Plains. See also Green Mountain Reservoir. Recreation is administered by Summit County. Located in north-central Colorado, north of Frisco. From I-70 near Silverthorne travel north on SH 9 for about 30 miles.

Recreation Contact: Summit County Government, Planning Division, P.O. Box 68, Breckenridge CO 80424 / 970-453-2561, ext. 115.

Green Mountain Reservoir

BOR Region: Great Plains. See also Green Mountain Camp. Recreation is administered by the U.S. Forest Service. Located in north central Colorado, north of Frisco. From I-70 near Silverthorne travel north on SH 9 for about 30 miles.

Recreation Contact: Arapaho National Forest, P.O. Box 620, Silverthorne CO 80498 / 970-468-5400.

Gunnison River Fishing Easements

BOR Region: Upper Colorado. See also Blue Mesa Reservoir. Recreation is administered by the State of Colorado. Located in west-central Colorado near Gunnison. From Gunnison, go north about 2 miles on SH 135 and watch for the Division of Wildlife signs. The area includes several stretches of the Gunnison River.

Recreation Contact: Colorado Division of Wildlife, Gunnison River Fishing Easements, 300 W New York Ave., Gunnison CO 81230 / 970-641-0088.

Horsethief Canyon State Wildlife Area

BOR Region: Upper Colorado. See also Colorado River Wildlife Area. Recreation is administered by the State of Colorado. Located in western Colorado, west of Grand Junction. From Fruita exit on I-70, go 1 mile south on SH 340 to property sign, take access road 4 miles to the reservoir. To reach the wildlife area travel south on SH 340 for 4 miles, turn west at King View Estates on County Road 1.3 and drive for about 2 miles.

Recreation Contact: Colorado Division of Wildlife, Horsethief Canyon SWA, P.O. Box 506, Fruita CO 81521 / 970-858-3200.

Horsetooth Reservoir

BOR Region: Great Plains. Recreation is administered by Larimer County. Located in northern Colorado, west of Ft. Collins. The southern portion of the reservoir is reached from Fort Collins by following Horsetooth Road west from the intersection with US 287. The northern end of the reservoir is reached from Bellvue by following CR 23 south.

Recreation Contact: Larimer County Parks Department, Horsetooth Reservoir, 1800 S County Road 31, Loveland CO 80537 / 970-679-4570.

Jackson Gulch Reservoir

BOR Region: Upper Colorado. Recreation is administered by the State of Colorado. Located in southwestern Colorado, northeast of Cortez. From Cortez follow US 160 to Mancos. Take SH 184 north about ¼-mile to County Road 42, then right. Follow CR 42 about 5 miles east to the junction of County Road N, turn left for ¼-mile to the state park entrance. The reservoir is located about 10 miles from Mesa Verde National Park.

Recreation Contact: Mancos State Park, P.O. Box 1697, Arboles CO 81121 / 970-883-2208.

Lake Estes

BOR Region: Great Plains. See also East Portal Reservoir and Mary's Lake. Recreation is administered by Estes Valley Recreation and Park District. Located in northern Colorado near the Rocky Mountain National Park. Lake Estes lies between US 34 and US 36 just east of downtown Estes Park.

Recreation Contact: Estes Valley Recreation and Park District, Lake Estes, P.O. Box 1379, Estes Park CO 80517 / 970-586-8191.

Lake Granby

BOR Region: Great Plains. See also Shadow Mountain Lake and Willow Creek Reservoir. Recreation is administered by the U.S. Forest Service. Located in northern Colorado near the Rocky Mountain National Park. The lake can be accessed north of Granby off US 34.

Recreation Contact: Arapaho National Forest, P.O. Box 10, Granby CO 80446 / 970-887-3331.

Lemon Reservoir

BOR Region: Upper Colorado. See also Vallecito Reservoir. Recreation is administered by the U.S. Forest Service. Located in southwestern Colorado, north of Durango. From Durango take CR 240 north to the intersection of CR 243, a distance of about 12 miles. Follow CR 243 (dirt road) north about 2 miles to Lemon Reservoir.

Recreation Contact: San Juan National Forest, Columbine Ranger District, 110 W 11th St., Durango CO 81301 / 970-884-2512.

Marys Lake

BOR Region: Great Plains. See also East Portal Reservoir and Lake Estes. Recreation is administered by Estes Valley Recreation and Park District. Located in northern Colorado near Rocky Mountain NP. Mary's Lake is a few miles south of downtown Estes Park, just west of SH 7. Follow Peak View Drive west 2 miles from the intersection with SH 7.

Recreation Contact: Estes Valley Recreation and Park District, Mary's Lake, P.O. Box 1379, Estes Park CO 80517 / 970-586-8191.

McPhee Reservoir

BOR Region: Upper Colorado. Recreation is administered by the U.S. Forest Service. Located in southwestern Colorado, north of Cortez. From US 160 near Cortez travel north on SH 145 to SH 184. Follow SH 184 west to County Road 25, turn right for ¼ mile, then right on Forest Service Road 271 to the reservoir.

Recreation Contact: San Juan National Forest, Mancos Dolores Ranger District, P.O. Box 210, Dolores CO 81323 / 970-882-7296.

Morrow Point Reservoir

BOR Region: Upper Colorado. See also Blue Mesa, Crawford, and Crystal Reservoirs. Recreation is administered by the National Park Service. No road access to reservoir. Access by foot trail only. Pine Creek Trail (2 miles, moderately strenuous) is located off US 50, 1 mile west of its Jct. with SH 92, 5.7 miles west of Jct. with US 50. Hermit's Rest Trail (6 miles, very strenuous) located off SH 92, 17 miles west of its Jct. with US 50. The Gunnison River below Morrow Point Dam may be reached by vehicle via Cimarron Drive north from Cimarron. Morrow Point is one of three reservoirs included as part of the Curecanti NRA.

Recreation Contact: National Park Service, Curecanti NRA, 102 Elk Creek, Gunnison CO 81230 / 970-641-2337.

Navajo Reservoir

BOR Region: Upper Colorado. Recreation is administered by the States of Colorado and New Mexico. Located in southwestern Colorado and northwestern New Mexico, about 45 miles southeast of Durango, Colorado. To reach the state recreation area in Colorado follow SH 151 south off US 160 near Chimney Rock. The recreation areas in New Mexico are accessed from SH 539 and 511 off US 64.

Recreation Contact: New Mexico Recreation Areas: Navajo Lake State Park, 1448 NM 511 #1, Navajo Dam NM 87419 / 505-632-2278. Colorado Recreation Areas: Navajo SRA, P.O. Box 1697, Arboles CO 81121 / 970-883-2208.

Paonia Reservoir

BOR Region: Upper Colorado. Recreation is administered by the State of Colorado. Located in west-central Colorado, about 50 miles south of Glenwood Springs. From Paonia, go north on SH 133 for about 13 miles to the reservoir.

Recreation Contact: Paonia State Park, P.O. Box 147, Crawford CO 81416 / 970-921-5721.

Pinewood Lake

BOR Region: Great Plains. See also Carter Lake and Flatiron Reservoir. Recreation is administered by Larimer County. Located in northern Colorado, west of Loveland. To reach Pinewood Lake from Loveland, follow US 36 west about 7 miles to CR 29. Follow CR 29 south 2 miles to CR 18E and turn west, follow to reservoir.

Recreation Contact: Larimer County Parks Department, Pinewood Lake, 1800 S County Road 31, Loveland CO 80537 / 970-679-4570.

Platoro Reservoir

BOR Region: Upper Colorado. Recreation is administered by the U.S. Forest Service. Located in southern Colorado, about 75 miles southwest of Alamosa. From Antonito, follow SH 17 west approximately 21 miles to Forest Service Road 250, then northwest about 23 miles to the reservoir.

Recreation Contact: Rio Grande National Forest, 21461 SH 285, La Jara CO 81140 / 719-274-5193.

Pueblo Reservoir

BOR Region: Great Plains. Recreation is administered by the State of Colorado. Located in central Colorado just west of Pueblo. From I-25 go west 4 miles on US 50, then south on Pueblo Blvd for 4 miles, then west 6 miles on Thatcher Avenue to the state recreation area.

Recreation Contact: Pueblo State Park, 640 Reservoir Rd., Pueblo CO 81005 / 719-561-9320.

Ridgway Reservoir

BOR Region: Upper Colorado. See also Silver Jack Reservoir. Recreation is administered by the State of Colorado. Located in southwestern Colorado, south of Montrose. The recreation area can be reached off US 550, 21 miles south of Montrose.

Recreation Contact: Ridgway State Park, 28555 Hwy. 550, Ridgway CO 81432 / 970-626-5822.

Rifle Gap Reservoir

BOR Region: Upper Colorado. Recreation is administered by the State of Colorado. Located in northwestern Colorado, northwest of Glenwood Springs. From Rifle off I-70 travel north on SH 13 to SH 325, then north on SH 325 for 10 miles to the reservoir.

Recreation Contact: Rifle Gap State Recreation Area, 0050 County Road 219, Rifle CO 81650 / 970-625-1607.

Ruedi Reservoir

BOR Region: Great Plains. Recreation is administered by the U.S. Forest Service. Located in west-central Colorado southeast of Glenwood Springs. From Glenwood Springs, follow SH 82 south for about 23 miles to Basalt. From Basalt, head east on Frying Pan Road (CR 4) approximately 13 miles to reservoir.

Recreation Contact: White River National Forest, P.O. Box 948, Glenwood Springs CO 81601 / 970-963-2266.

Shadow Mountain Lake

BOR Region: Great Plains. See also Lake Granby and Willow Creek Reservoir. Recreation is administered by the U.S. Forest Service. Located in north-central Colorado, just west of Rocky Mountain National Park. Shadow Mountain Lake lies adjacent to Grand Lake, east of US 34 near the western entrance to the national park.

Recreation Contact: Arapaho National Forest, Sulphur Ranger District, P.O. Box 10, Granby CO 80446 / 970-887-3331.

Silver Jack Reservoir

BOR Region: Upper Colorado. See also Blue Mesa and Ridgway Reservoirs. Recreation is administered by the U.S. Forest Service. Located in western Colorado, south of Montrose. From Montrose, follow US 50 east about 22 miles to Cimarron Road. Turn south on Cimarron Road and follow approximately 10 miles to the national forest boundary. Cimarron Road then becomes Forest Service Road 858. Follow FSR 858 south about 8 miles to the reservoir.

Recreation Contact: Uncompahgre National Forest, Ouray Ranger District, 2505 S. Townsend, Montrose CO 81401 / 970-249-3711.

Taylor Park Reservoir

BOR Region: Upper Colorado. See also Taylor River State wildlife Area. Recreation is administered by the U.S. Forest Service. Located in central Colorado, northeast of Gunnison. From Gunnison travel 11 miles north on SH 135 to Forest Service Road 742, then 19 miles east to the reservoir. Winter access can be icy and snowpacked.

Recreation Contact: Gunnison National Forest, Taylor River Ranger District, 216 N Colorado, Gunnison CO 81230 / 970-641-0471.

Taylor River State Wildlife Area

BOR Region: Upper Colorado. See also Taylor Park Reservoir. Recreation is administered by the State of Colorado. Located in central

Colorado, northeast of Gunnison. From Gunnison travel 11 miles north on SH 135 to Forest Service Road 742, then 19 miles east to the base of Taylor Dam. Watch for the Division of Wildlife signs. Winter access can be icy and snowpacked.

Recreation Contact: Colorado Division of Wildlife, Taylor River SWA, 300 W New York Ave., Gunnison CO 81230 / 970-641-0088.

Turquoise Lake

BOR Region: Great Plains. Recreation is administered by the U.S. Forest Service. Located in central Colorado, about 4 miles west of Leadville. Follow Mountain View Drive west from Leadville to the lake.

Recreation Contact: White River National Forest, 2015 North Poplar, Leadville CO 80461 / 719-486-0749.

Twin Lakes Reservoir

BOR Region: Great Plains. Recreation is administered by the U.S. Forest Service. Located in central Colorado, about 13 miles south of Leadville. The lakes can be accessed 2 miles west of US 24 on SH 82.

Recreation Contact: White River National Forest, 2015 N Poplar, Leadville CO 80461 / 719-486-0749.

Vallecito Reservoir

BOR Region: Upper Colorado. See also Lemon Reservoir. Recreation is administered by the U.S. Forest Service and Pine River Irrigation District. Located in southwestern Colorado, northeast of Durango. From Durango, take County Road 240 north for about 14 miles to the intersection of County Road 501. Turn left (north) on County Road 501 to the reservoir, a distance of about 4 miles.

Recreation Contact: Pine River Irrigation District, 13029 County Rd. 501, Bayfield CO 81122 / 970-884-2558. San Juan National Forest, Columbine Ranger District, 110 W. 11th St., Durango CO 81301 / 970-884-2512.

Vega Reservoir

BOR Region: Upper Colorado. See also Bonham and Cottonwood #1 Reservoirs. Recreation is administered by the State of Colorado. Located in western Colorado, east of Grand Junction. From I-70 follow SH 65 east to SH 330, continue east another 11 miles to Collbran. From Collbram follow the signs an additional 12 miles east to the reservoir.

Recreation Contact: Vega State Park, P.O. Box 186, Collbran CO 81624 / 970-487-3407.

Willow Creek Reservoir

BOR Region: Great Plains. Recreation is administered by the U.S. Forest Service. Located in north-central Colorado approximately 9 miles north of Granby. From Granby follow US 40 west to US 34. Follow US 34 north about 5 miles to CR 40 and travel west about 3 miles to the lake.

Recreation Contact: Arapaho National Forest, P.O. Box 10, Granby CO 80446 / 970-887-3331.

Primary Game Fish

	Bass	Bluegill	Catfish	Crappie	Pike	Perch	Salmon	Trout	Walleye
1 Blue Mesa Reservoir							•	•	
2 Bonham Reservoir								•	
3 Bonny Reservoir	•	•	•	•	•				•
4 Carter Lake	•						•	•	
5 Colorado River Wildlife Area	•	•	•	•				•	
6 Cottonwood #1 Reservoir								•	
7 Crawford Reservoir	•		•	•	•	•		•	
8 Crystal Reservoir							•	•	
9 East Portal Reservoir								•	
10 Flatiron Reservoir	•						•	•	
11 Fruitgrowers Reservoir		•		•		•			

Primary Game Fish *(continued)*

	Bass	Bluegill	Catfish	Crappie	Pike	Perch	Salmon	Trout	Walleye
12 Green Mountain Camp							•	•	
13 Green Mountain Reservoir							•	•	
14 Gunnison River								•	
15 Horsethief Canyon SWA	•		•	•		•		•	•
16 Horsetooth Reservoir	•							•	•
17 Jackson Gulch Reservoir	•						•	•	
18 Lake Estes								•	
19 Lake Granby							•	•	
20 Lemon Reservoir							•	•	
21 Marys Lake								•	
22 McPhee Reservoir	•	•	•	•		•	•	•	
23 Morrow Point Reservoir							•	•	
24 Navajo Reservoir	•		•		•		•	•	
25 Paonia Reservoir						•		•	
26 Pinewood Lake	•						•	•	
27 Platoro Reservoir								•	
28 Pueblo Reservoir	•			•	•	•	•		•
29 Ridgway Reservoir							•	•	
30 Rifle Gap Reservoir	•	•	•			•		•	•
31 Ruedi Reservoir								•	
32 Shadow Mountain Lake							•	•	
33 Silver Jack Reservoir								•	
34 Taylor Park Reservoir							•	•	
35 Taylor River SWA								•	
36 Turquoise Lake								•	
37 Twin Lakes Reservoir								•	
38 Vallecito Reservoir					•		•	•	•
39 Vega Reservoir								•	
40 Willow Creek Reservoir							•	•	

IDAHO

1 American Falls Reservoir
2 Anderson Ranch Reservoir
3 Arrowrock Reservoir
4 Black Canyon Reservoir
5 Cascade Reservoir
6 Deadwood Reservoir
7 Island Park Reservoir
8 Lake Lowell
9 Lake Waha

10 Lake Walcott
11 Little Wood River Reservoir
12 Mann Creek Reservoir
13 Mann Lake Reservoir A
14 Montour Wildlife / Recreation
    Management Area
15 Palisades Reservoir
16 Ririe Reservoir
17 Soldiers Meadow Reservoir

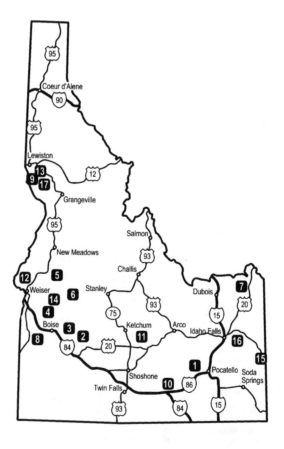

Activities and Facilities

#	Camping	Wildlife	Boating	Fishing	Hiking	Swimming	Picnicking	Boat Launch	Restrooms	Information	Accessible
1	•	•	•	•		•	•	•	•	•	
2	•	•	•	•	•	•	•	•	•		
3	•	•	•	•		•			•		
4	•	•	•	•		•	•		•		•
5	•	•	•	•	•	•	•	•	•		•
6	•	•	•	•	•	•	•		•		
7	•	•	•	•		•	•	•	•		
8		•	•	•			•		•		
9	•	•	•			•	•				
10	•	•	•	•	•	•	•		•		
11	•	•	•	•		•	•		•		
12	•	•	•	•		•	•		•		
13		•									
14	•	•		•	•		•		•		
15	•	•	•		•	•	•		•		
16	•	•	•	•		•	•		•	•	
17	•	•	•	•		•	•		•		

American Falls Reservoir

BOR Region: Pacific Northwest. Recreation is administered by the Bureau of Reclamation, Bingham County, and the City of American Falls. Located in southeastern Idaho west of Pocatello and north of American Falls. Numerous access points are available along I-86 and SH 39.

Recreation Contact: Bureau of Reclamation, Snake River Area Office, 214 Broadway Ave., Boise ID 83702 / 208-334-1460. Bingham County, P.O. Box 725, Blackfoot ID 83221 / 208-785-4440. American Falls Chamber of Commerce, P.O. Box 207, American Falls ID 83211 / 208-226-7214.

Anderson Ranch Reservoir

BOR Region: Pacific Northwest. Recreation is administered by the U.S. Forest Service. Located in southwestern Idaho, southeast of Boise near Mountain Home. From Mountain Home travel about 20 miles east on US 20 to Anderson Ranch Dam Road, head north to reservoir. Additional access around the reservoir is from the Anderson Dam or Fall Creek improved dirt roads.

Recreation Contact: Boise National Forest, 1249 S Vinnell Way, Boise ID 83709 / 208-373-4007.

Arrowrock Reservoir

BOR Region: Pacific Northwest. Recreation is administered by the U.S. Forest Service. Located in southwest Idaho, about 20 miles east of Boise. To reach the reservoir from I-84, follow SH 21 east for about 18 miles to Mores Creek Bridge. Take the road to the right to Arrowrock Dam.

Recreation Contact: Boise National Forest, 1249 S Vinnell Way, Boise ID 83709 / 208-373-4007.

Black Canyon Reservoir

BOR Region: Pacific Northwest. See also Montour Wildlife / Recreation Management Area. Recreation is administered by the Bureau of Reclamation. Located about 35 miles northwest of Boise, in western Idaho near Emmett. To reach the reservoir travel west on SH 52 off SH 55 in Horseshoe Bend, Idaho.

Recreation Contact: Bureau of Reclamation, Snake River Area Office, 214 Broadway Ave., Boise ID 83702 / 208-334-1460.

Cascade Reservoir

BOR Region: Pacific Northwest. Recreation is administered by the State of Idaho. Located in western Idaho about 70 miles north of Boise. The reservoir is west of Cascade, off SH 55. An improved dirt road travels around the perimeter.

Recreation Contact: Idaho Department of Parks and Recreation, P.O. Box 83720, Boise ID 83712 / 208-334-4180.

Deadwood Reservoir

BOR Region: Pacific Northwest. Recreation is administered by the U.S. Forest Service. Located in west-central Idaho, northeast of Boise. To reach the reservoir from Lowman, follow Garden Valley Road west about 10 miles to Scott Mountain Road. Follow Scott Mountain Road north approximately 24 miles to the reservoir. The reservoir can also be reached from Cascade by following Warm Lake Road about 24 miles to Landmark Stanley Road, then south about 17 miles to FSR 555. Follow FSR 555 south 8 miles to reservoir.

Recreation Contact: Boise National Forest, 1249 S Vinnell Way, Boise ID 83709 / 208-373-4007.

Island Park Reservoir

BOR Region: Pacific Northwest. Recreation is administered by the U.S. Forest Service. Located in the high country of eastern Idaho, north of Idaho Falls, near Montana and Wyoming state lines. The reservoir is located immediately west of US 20, near Island Park, Idaho.

Recreation Contact: Targhee National Forest, 420 Bridge St., Saint Anthony ID 83445 / 208-624-3151.

Lake Lowell

BOR Region: Pacific Northwest. Recreation is administered by the U.S. Fish and Wildlife Service. Located in western Idaho, near the Oregon border, 5 miles southwest of Nampa. From 12th Street in downtown Nampa go south to Lake Lowell Avenue, turn right and continue west four miles.

Recreation Contact: U.S. Fish and Wildlife Service, Deer Flat National Wildlife Refuge, 13751 Upper Embankment Road, Nampa ID 83686 / 208-467-9278.

Lake Waha

BOR Region: Pacific Northwest. See also Mann Lake Reservoir A and Soldiers Meadow Reservoir. Recreation is administered by the Lewiston Orchards Irrigation District. Located in western Idaho, southeast of Lewiston. From Lewiston, follow Thain Road southeast to Waha Road. Turn south on Waha Road and follow about 10 miles to the lake.

Recreation Contact: Lewiston Orchards Irrigation District, 1520 Powers Avenue, Lewiston ID 83501 / 208-746-8235.

Lake Walcott

BOR Region: Pacific Northwest. Recreation is administered by the U.S. Fish and Wildlife Service and State of Idaho. Located in south-central Idaho, about 5 miles east of Rupert, within the Minidoka National Wildlife Refuge. To reach the refuge headquarters from Rupert, follow SH 24 north 6 miles to CR 400 and turn east. Follow CR 400 east about 6 miles.

Recreation Contact: Idaho Department of Parks and Recreation, P.O. Box 83720, Boise ID 83712 / 208-334-4180. U.S. Fish and Wildlife Service, Minidoka National Wildlife Refuge, Route 4 Box 290, Rupert ID 83350 / 208-267-3888.

Little Wood River Reservoir

BOR Region: Pacific Northwest. Recreation is administered by the Bureau of Reclamation. Located in south-central Idaho, about 13 miles north of Carey. To reach the lake, follow US 20 north about 3 miles to High Line Road. Head north on High Line Road about 1 mile to Barton Road and turn west. Follow Barton Road northwest to the reservoir. The reservoir can also be reached from Bellevue by following Muldoon Canyon Road east approximately 17 miles.

Recreation Contact: Bureau of Reclamation, Snake River Area Office, 214 Broadway Ave., Boise ID 83702 / 208-334-1460.

Mann Creek Reservoir

BOR Region: Pacific Northwest. Recreation is administered by the Bureau of Reclamation. Located in western Idaho, north of Weiser. To reach the reservoir from Weiser, follow US 95 north approximately 13 miles to Upper Mann Creek Road. Follow Upper Mann Creek Road west about 1 mile to reservoir.

Recreation Contact: Bureau of Reclamation, Snake River Area Office, 214 Broadway Avenue, Boise ID 83702 / 208-334-1460.

Mann Lake Reservoir A

BOR Region: Pacific Northwest. See also Lake Waha and Soldiers Meadow Reservoir. Recreation is administered by Lewiston Orchards Irrigation District. Located in western Idaho, southeast of Lewiston. From Lewiston Orchards, follow Powers Avenue east about 5 miles to the reservoir.

Recreation Contact: Lewiston Orchards Irrigation District, 1520 Powers Ave., Lewiston ID 83501 / 208-746-8235.

Montour Wildlife / Recreation Management Area

BOR Region: Pacific Northwest. See also Black Canyon Reservoir. Recreation is administered by the Bureau of Reclamation. Located northeast of Emmett in southwestern Idaho. Access is via SH 52. This complex of wetlands and ponds cover 1,105 acres and is located above Black Canyon Reservoir.

Recreation Contact: Bureau of Reclamation, Snake River Area Office, 214 Broadway Ave., Boise ID 83702 / 208-334-1460.

Palisades Reservoir

BOR Region: Pacific Northwest. Recreation is administered by the U.S. Forest Service. Located in eastern Idaho and western Wyoming, east of Idaho Falls near Alpine, Wyoming. Access is available along US 26, south of Palisades, Idaho.

Recreation Contact: Targhee National Forest, 420 Bridge St., Saint Anthony ID 83445 / 208-624-3151.

Ririe Reservoir

BOR Region: Pacific Northwest. Recreation is administered by Bonneville County. Located in eastern Idaho, northeast of Idaho Falls. To reach the area from Idaho Falls, follow US 26 northeast about 16 miles to Meadow Creek Road. Follow Meadow Creek Road south about 2 miles to the reservoir.

Recreation Contact: Bonnevile County Parks & Recreation Dept., 605 N Capitol, Idaho Falls ID 83402 / 208-538-7285.

Soldiers Meadow Reservoir

BOR Region: Pacific Northwest. See also Lake Waha and Mann Lake Reservoir A. Recreation is administered by Lewiston Orchards Irrigation District. Located in western Idaho, 14 miles southwest of Winchester. To reach the reservoir from Winchester, follow Woodside Road south to Morrowtown Road. Head west on Morrowtown Road about 7 miles to the reservoir.

Recreation Contact: Lewiston Orchards Irrigation District, 1520 Powers Avenue, Lewiston ID 83501 / 208-746-8235.

Primary Game Fish

	BASS	BLUEGILL	CATFISH	CRAPPIE	PIKE	PERCH	SALMON	TROUT	WALLEYE
1 American Falls Reservoir			•	•	•		•	•	•
2 Anderson Ranch Reservoir	•						•	•	•
3 Arrowrock Reservoir							•	•	•
4 Black Canyon Reservoir	•			•	•				•
5 Cascade Reservoir	•			•	•		•	•	•
6 Deadwood Reservoir								•	•
7 Island Park Reservoir			•				•	•	•
8 Lake Lowell	•	•	•	•			•		•
9 Lake Waha	•								•
10 Lake Walcott	•				•		•		•
11 Little Wood River Reservoir									•
12 Mann Creek Reservoir	•				•				•
13 Mann Lake Reservoir A	•				•				•
14 Montour Wildlife / RMA	•								•
15 Palisades Reservoir								•	•
16 Ririe Reservoir									•
17 Soldiers Meadow Reservoir								•	•

Kansas

1 Cedar Bluff Reservoir
2 Cheney Reservoir
3 Keith Sebeluis Reservoir
4 Kirwin NWR

5 Lovewell Reservoir
6 Waconda Reservoir
7 Webster Reservoir
8 Woodston Diversion Dam

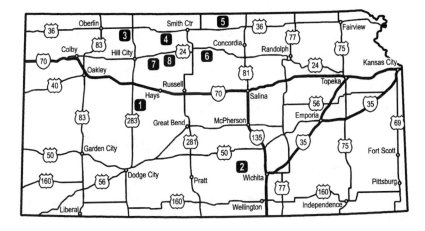

Activities and Facilities

	🏕	🚤	🛶	🎣	🥾	🏊	⛽	⚓	🚻	ℹ	♿
1	•	•	•	•	•	•	•	•	•	•	•
2	•	•	•	•	•	•	•	•	•		•
3	•	•	•	•		•	•		•	•	
4	•	•	•	•	•	•	•	•	•	•	•
5	•	•	•	•		•	•	•	•	•	
6	•	•	•	•	•	•	•	•	•	•	
7	•	•	•	•	•	•	•		•	•	•
8		•		•							

Cedar Bluff Reservoir

BOR Region: Great Plains. Recreation is administered by the State of Kansas. Located in west-central Kansas, about 20 miles south of Wakeeney. From Wakeeney, follow I-70 east about 8 miles to SH 147, then south about 13 miles to the reservoir.

Recreation Contact: Cedar Bluff State Park, Rt 2 Box 76A, Ellis KS 67637 / 785-726-3212.

Cheney Reservoir

BOR Region: Great Plains. Recreation is administered by the State of Kansas. Located in south-central Kansas, west of Wichita. The reservoir is accessed from several routes including SH 17 and 251, both off US 54.

Recreation Contact: Cheney State Park, 16000 NE 50th St., Cheney KS 67025 / 316-542-3664.

Keith Sebeluis Reservoir

BOR Region: Great Plains. Recreation is administered by the State of Kansas. Located in northwestern Kansas, 4 miles southwest of Norton. The reservoir can be accessed off US 36 or US 283. The Norton Wildlife Area surrounds the lake.

Recreation Contact: Prairie Dog State Park, Box 431, Norton KS 67654 / 785-877-2953.

![icons]

Kirwin National Wildlife Refuge

BOR Region: Great Plains. Recreation is administered by the U.S. Fish and Wildlife Service. Located in northern Kansas about 5 miles southeast of Philipsburg. From Philipsburg travel south on US 183, then east on SH9 to the reservoir.

Recreation Contact: U.S. Fish and Wildlife Service, Kirwin National Wildlife Refuge, Rt 1 Box 103, Kirwin KS 67644 / 785-543-6673.

Lovewell Reservoir

BOR Region: Great Plains. Recreation is administered by the State of Kansas. Located in northern Kansas, northwest of Concordia, Kansas and 10 miles south of Superior, Nebraska. The reservoir can be accessed off US 36 on SH 14.

Recreation Contact: Lovewell State Park, RR 1 Box 66A, Webber KS 66970 / 785-753-4971.

Waconda Reservoir

BOR Region: Great Plains. Recreation is administered by the State of Kansas. Located in north-central Kansas, about 17 miles west of Beloit. There are several access roads for the reservoir including US 24 and SH 181.

Recreation Contact: Glen Elder State Park, Rt 1 Box 162A, Glen Elder KS 67446 / 785-545-3345.

Webster Reservoir

BOR Region: Great Plains. See also Woodston Diversion Dam. Recreation is administered by the State of Kansas. Located in north-central Kansas, about 10 miles west of Stockton off US 24.

Recreation Contact: Webster State Park, 1210 Nine Road, Stockton KS 67669 / 785-425-6775.

Woodston Diversion Dam

BOR Region: Great Plains. See also Webster Reservoir. Recreation is administered by the State of Kansas. Located in north-central Kansas, about 7 miles east of Stockton along US 24. This area is managed by the Kansas Department of Wildlife & Parks as a wildlife management area.

Recreation Contact: Kansas Department of Wildlife and Parks, Woodston Diversion Wildlife Area, P.O. Box 338, Hays KS 67601 / 785-628-8614.

Primary Game Fish

	Bass	Bluegill	Catfish	Crappie	Pike	Perch	Salmon	Trout	Walleye
1 Cedar Bluff Reservoir	•		•	•					•
2 Cheney Reservoir	•		•	•					•
3 Keith Sebeluis Reservoir	•		•	•					•
4 Kirwin NWR			•	•					•
5 Lovewell Reservoir	•		•	•					•
6 Waconda Reservoir	•		•	•					•
7 Webster Reservoir	•	•	•	•				•	•
8 Woodston Diversion Dam	•	•	•	•					•

MONTANA

1 Bighorn Canyon NRA
2 Canyon Ferry Lake
3 Clark Canyon Reservoir
4 Fresno Reservoir
5 Gibson Reservoir
6 Helena Valley Reservoir

7 Hungry Horse Reservoir
8 Lake Elwell
9 Nelson Reservoir
10 Pishkun Reservoir
11 Willow Creek Reservoir

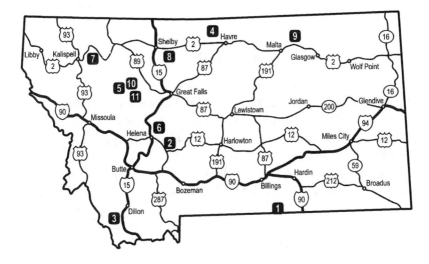

Activities and Facilities

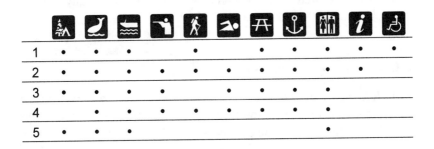

	🏕	🚤	🛶	🎣	🥾	🏊	🪑	⚓	🚻	i	♿
1	•		•		•			•	•	•	•	•
2	•	•	•	•	•	•	•	•	•	•	
3	•	•	•	•		•	•	•	•		
4		•	•	•	•	•	•	•	•		
5	•	•	•						•		

Activities and Facilities *(continued)*

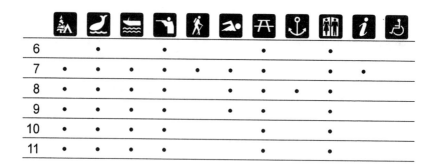

	1	2	3	4	5	6	7	8	9	10	11
6		•		•			•		•		
7	•	•	•	•	•	•	•		•	•	
8	•	•	•	•		•	•	•	•		
9	•	•	•	•		•			•		
10	•	•	•	•			•		•		
11	•	•	•	•			•		•		

Bighorn Canyon National Recreation Area

BOR Region: Great Plains. Recreation is administered by the National Park Service. Located in southern Montana and northern Wyoming, west of I-90. In Wyoming the area is accessed off US Alt 14 near Lovell. In Montana several secondary state highways, including 313 and 463, lead to the recreation area.

Recreation Contact: National Park Service, Bighorn Canyon NRA, Box 7458, Fort Smith MT 59035 / 406-666-2412.

Canyon Ferry Lake

BOR Region: Great Plains. See also Helena Valley Reservoir. Recreation is administered by the Bureau of Land Management and Bureau of Reclamation. Located in central Montana, east of Helena. From Townsend the lake can be accessed off US 12 or US 287.

Recreation Contact: Canyon Ferry Visitor Center, 7661 Canyon Ferry Road, Helena MT 59601 / 406-475-3319.

Clark Canyon Reservoir

BOR Region: Great Plains. Recreation is administered by the Bureau of Reclamation. Located in southwestern Montana, about 20 miles south of Dillon. The reservoir can be accessed off I-15. The Lewis and Clark

Memorial is near the north end of the reservoir.

Recreation Contact: Bureau of Reclamation, 1100 Highway 41, Dillon MT 59725 / 406-683-6472.

Fresno Reservoir

BOR Region: Great Plains. Recreation is administered by the Bureau of Reclamation. Located in northern Montana, about 12 miles west of Havre. The reservoir is accessed from either US 2 or SH 232.

Recreation Contact: Bureau of Reclamation, Montana Area Office, P.O. Box 30173, Billings MT 59107 / 406-247-6075.

Gibson Reservoir

BOR Region: Great Plains. See also Pishkun and Willow Creek Reservoirs. Recreation is administered by the U.S. Forest Service. Located in west-central Montana, west of Great Falls and US 287 in the Lewis and Clark National Forest. The reservoir can be reached from August on US 287 by following Sun Canyon Road northeast about 23 miles.

Recreation Contact: Lewis and Clark National Forest, P.O. Box 871, Great Falls MT 59403 / 406-791-7700.

Helena Valley Reservoir

BOR Region: Great Plains. See also Canyon Ferry Lake. Recreation is administered by the State of Montana. Located in west-central Montana, northeast of Helena. To reach the reservoir from I-15 in Helena, take the Cedar Street exit and go east to Washington Street. Follow Washington Street north to Custer Avenue and turn east. Follow Custer Avenue east about 1 mile to York Road, then northeast about 6 miles to the reservoir.

Recreation Contact: Montana Fish, Wildlife and Parks, Helena Valley Reservoir, 930 Custer Avenue West, Helena MT 59601 / 406-449-8864.

Hungry Horse Reservoir

BOR Region: Pacific Northwest. Recreation is administered by the U.S. Forest Service. Located in northwestern Montana, about 25 miles east of Kalispell. The lake lies south of US 2 and the community of Hungry Horse. Forest Service Road 895 (West Side Road) follows the lake's western shore while FSR 38 (East Side Road) follows the eastern.

Recreation Contact: Flathead National Forest, Hungry Horse Ranger District, P.O. Box 340, Hungry Horse MT 59919 / 406-387-3800.

Lake Elwell

BOR Region: Great Plains. Recreation is administered by the Bureau of Reclamation. Located in northern Montana, east of Shelby. Several access roads for the northern portion of the lake are available off US 2. The southern portion of the lake can be reached off I-15 on state route 366. The lake is also known as Tiber Reservoir.

Recreation Contact: Bureau of Reclamation, P.O. Box 220, Chester MT 59522 / 406-456-3226.

Nelson Reservoir

BOR Region: Great Plains. Recreation is administered by the Bureau of Reclamation. Located in northern Montana off US 2, about 6 miles west of Saco.

Recreation Contact: Bureau of Reclamation, Montana Area Office, P.O. Box 30137, Billings MT 59107 / 406-247-6075.

Pishkun Reservoir

BOR Region: Great Plains. See also Gibson and Willow Creek Reservoirs. Recreation is administered by the State of Montana. Located in central Montana, west of Great Falls. To reach the reservoir from Augusta, follow US 287 north about 9 miles to the Pishkun Access Road and go north approximately 12 miles.

Recreation Contact: Montana Fish, Wildlife and Parks, Pishkun Reservoir, 4600 Giant Springs Road, Great Falls MT 59406 / 406-454-5840.

Willow Creek Reservoir

BOR Region: Great Plains. See also Gibson and Pishkun Reservoirs. Recreation is administered by the State of Montana. Located in central Montana, about 20 miles west of Great Falls. From August on US 287, follow Sun Canyon Road northwest approximately 6 miles to the reservoir.

Recreation Contact: Montana Fish, Wildlife and Parks, Willow Creek Reservoir, 4600 Giant Springs Road, Great Falls MT 59406 / 406-454-5840.

Primary Game Fish

	BASS	BLUEGILL	CATFISH	CRAPPIE	PIKE	PERCH	SALMON	TROUT	WALLEYE
1 Bighorn Canyon NRA			•			•		•	•
2 Canyon Ferry Lake						•		•	•
3 Clark Canyon Reservoir								•	
4 Fresno Reservoir					•	•			•
5 Gibson Reservoir								•	
6 Helena Valley Reservoir									
7 Hungry Horse Reservoir								•	
8 Lake Elwell					•	•		•	•
9 Nelson Reservoir					•	•			•
10 Pishkun Reservoir					•	•		•	
11 Willow Creek Reservoir								•	

Nebraska

1 Box Butte Reservoir
2 Calamus Reservoir
3 Davis Creek Reservoir
4 Enders Reservoir
5 Harry Strunk Reservoir

6 Hugh Butler Reservoir
7 Lake Minatare SRA
8 Merritt Reservoir
9 Sherman Reservoir
10 Swanson Reservoir
11 Winters Creek Lake

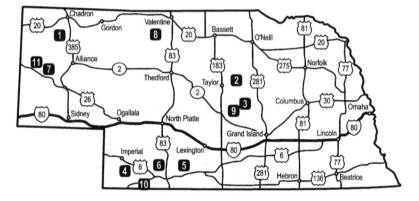

Activities and Facilities

	Camping	Wildlife	Boating	Fishing	Hiking	Swimming	Picnic	Marina	Restrooms	Information	Accessible
1	•	•	•	•		•	•		•		
2	•	•	•	•		•	•		•	•	•
3	•	•	•						•		
4	•	•	•	•		•	•		•		
5	•	•	•	•		•	•	•	•		
6	•	•	•	•	•	•	•	•	•	•	
7	•	•	•		•		•		•	•	
8	•	•	•	•		•	•	•	•	•	
9	•	•	•	•		•	•	•	•		
10	•	•	•	•	•	•	•	•	•	•	
11		•	•								

Box Butte Reservoir

BOR Region: Great Plains. Recreation is administered by the State of Nebraska. Located in northwestern Nebraska, south of Chadron and 10 miles north of Hemingford. Box Butte Reservoir is reached from Chadron by following US 385 south 26 miles to Dunlap Road. Turn west on Dunlap Road and travel about 5 miles to the reservoir.

Recreation Contact: Box Butte SRA, Box 30370, Lincoln NE 68503 / 402-762-5605.

Calamus Reservoir

BOR Region: Great Plains. Recreation is administered by the State of Nebraska. Located in central Nebraska, about 25 miles northwest of Ord. Calamus Reservoir is reached from Burwell on SH 11 by traveling 6 miles northwest on the Calamus Dam Road.

Recreation Contact: Calamus Reservoir SRA, HC 79 Box 20L, Burwell NE 68823 / 308-346-5666.

Davis Creek Reservoir

BOR Region: Great Plains. See also Sherman Reservoir. Recreation is administered by the Bureau of Reclamation. Located in central Nebraska, about 20 miles south of Ord. The reservoir is reached from SH 22 near North Loup by traveling south on Ashton Highway for 6 miles.

Recreation Contact: Davis Creek Reservoir, Box 129, Ord NE 68862 / 308-745-0230.

Enders Reservoir

BOR Region: Great Plains. Recreation is administered by the State of Nebraska. Located in southwestern Nebraska, south of Imperial near the community of Enders. Enders Reservoir is located near the intersection of US 6 and SH 61 about 10 miles southeast of Imperial.

Recreation Contact: Enders Reservoir SRA, RR 1 Box 4B, Enders NE 69027 / 308-394-5118.

Harry Strunk Reservoir

BOR Region: Great Plains. Recreation is administered by the State of Nebraska. Located in southern Nebraska, about 30 miles northeast of McCook and 9 miles northwest of Cambridge. To reach the reservoir from Cambridge, follow US 6 west about 3 miles to Harry Strunk Lake Road. Turn north and follow Harry Strunk Lake Road for 6 miles.

Recreation Contact: Medicine Creek SRA, RR 2 Box 95, Cambridge NE 69022 / 308-697-4667.

Hugh Butler Reservoir

BOR Region: Great Plains. Recreation is administered by the State of Nebraska. Located in southern Nebraska about 10 miles north of McCook. The reservoir is accessed from US 83.

Recreation Contact: Red Willow SRA, RR 1 Box 145, McCook NE 69001 / 308-345-5899.

Lake Minatare State Recreation Area

BOR Region: Great Plains. See also Winters Creek Lake. Recreation is administered by the State of Nebraska. Located in western Nebraska, about 12 miles northeast of Scottsbluff. Lake Minatare is reached from the community of Minatare by traveling north on Stonegate Road (CR 30) for 7 miles.

Recreation Contact: Lake Minatare SRA, P.O. Box 188, Minatare NE 69356 / 308-783-2911.

Merritt Reservoir

BOR Region: Great Plains. Recreation is administered by the State of Nebraska. Located in northern Nebraska, about 21 miles southwest of Valentine. To reach Merritt Reservoir from US 20 near Valentine, travel south on SH 97 approximately 25 miles. The lake lies west of the state highway.

Recreation Contact: Merritt Reservoir SRA, 420 East First St., Valentine NE 69201 / 402-684-2921.

Sherman Reservoir

BOR Region: Great Plains. See also Davis Creek Reservoir. Recreation is administered by the State of Nebraska. Located in central Nebraska, northwest of Grand Island, about 5 miles east of Loup City. To reach the reservoir from Loup City, follow "N" Street east about 4 miles. The lake can also be reached from SH 92 east of Loup City by following access roads north.

Recreation Contact: Sherman Reservoir SRA, RR 2 Box 117, Loup City NE 68853 / 308-745-0230.

Swanson Reservoir

BOR Region: Great Plains. Recreation is administered by the State of Nebraska. Swanson Reservoir is located in southern Nebraska about 3 miles west of Trenton. The northern shore can be reached by following access roads south from US 34. The southern shore is reached from Trenton by following SH 25 southwest.

Recreation Contact: Swanson Reservoir SRA, RR 2 Box 20, Stratton NE 69043 / 308-276-2671.

Winters Creek Lake

BOR Region: Great Plains. See also Lake Minatare SRA. Recreation is administered by the U.S. Fish and Wildlife Service. Located in western Nebraska about 10 miles north of Scottsbluff. Located just west of Lake Minatare. It can be reached from the community of Minatare by traveling north on Stonegate Road about 7 miles.

Recreation Contact: North Platte National Wildlife Refuge, Box 1346, Scottsbluff NE 69363 / 308-635-7851.

Primary Game Fish

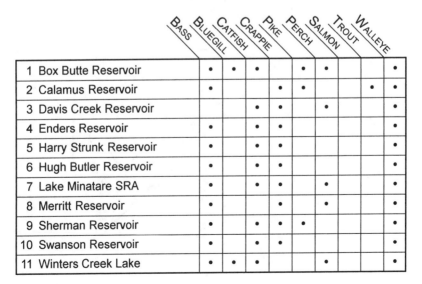

	BASS	BLUEGILL	CATFISH	CRAPPIE	PIKE	PERCH	SALMON	TROUT	WALLEYE
1 Box Butte Reservoir	•	•	•		•	•			•
2 Calamus Reservoir	•			•	•			•	•
3 Davis Creek Reservoir			•	•		•			•
4 Enders Reservoir	•		•	•					•
5 Harry Strunk Reservoir	•		•	•					•
6 Hugh Butler Reservoir	•		•	•					•
7 Lake Minatare SRA	•		•	•		•			•
8 Merritt Reservoir	•			•		•			•
9 Sherman Reservoir	•		•	•	•				•
10 Swanson Reservoir	•		•	•					•
11 Winters Creek Lake	•	•	•			•			•

Nevada

1   Davis Dam — Lake Mohave
2   Hoover Dam
3   Lahontan Reservoir
4   Lake Mead NRA
5   Lake Tahoe
6   Rye Patch Reservoir

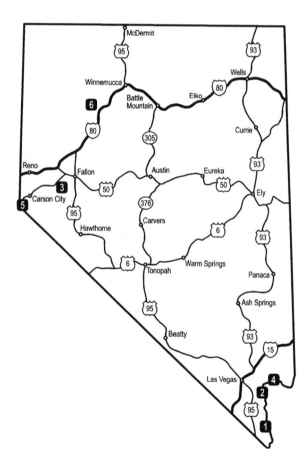

Activities and Facilities

	🏕	🦢	🚣	🎣	🚶	🏊	⛱	⚓	🚻	ℹ	♿
1	•	•	•		•	•	•	•	•	•	•
2					•				•	•	•
3	•	•	•			•	•		•	•	
4	•	•	•	•	•	•	•	•	•	•	•
5	•	•	•		•	•	•	•	•	•	•
6	•	•	•	•		•	•		•		•

Davis Dam — Lake Mohave

BOR Region: Lower Colorado. See also Hoover Dam and Lake Mead NRA. Recreation is administered by two county agencies and the National Park Service. Located 10 miles north of Bullhead City, on the Arizona side and 8 miles north of Laughlin, on the Nevada side of the Colorado River. From Bullhead City, travel north on SH 95 to Lake Mohave. Lake Mohave is part of the Lake Mead National Recreation Area administered by the National Park Service.

Recreation Contact: Mohave County Parks Department, P.O. Box 390, Kingman AZ 86402 / 602-757-0915. Clark County Parks and Recreation, 304 S 3rd St. Suite 220, Las Vegas NV 89155 / 702-455-8298.

Hoover Dam

BOR Region: Lower Colorado. See also Lake Mead NRA and Davis Dam—Lake Mohave. Hoover Dam is administered by the Bureau of Reclamation. Located in northwest Arizona and southeast Nevada on US 93. To reach Hoover Dam from Kingman, Arizona travel north on US 93. From Las Vegas, Nevada travel 30 miles southeast on US 93/95.

Recreation Contact: Bureau of Reclamation, Lower Colorado Region, P.O. Box 61470, Boulder City NV 89006 / 702-294-3513.

Lahontan Reservoir

BOR Region: Mid-Pacific. Recreation is administered by the State of Nevada. Located in western Nevada about 45 miles east of Carson City near Silver Springs. Reservoir access is provided along US 50.

Recreation Contact: Lahontan State Recreation Area, 16799 Lahontan Dam, Fallon NV 89406 / 702-867-3001.

Lake Mead National Recreation Area

BOR Region: Lower Colorado. See also Davis Dam—Lake Mohave and Hoover Dam. The National Park Service manages all the resources within the NRA boundaries. Located in northwestern Arizona and southeast Nevada. This large area can be accessed from several points off I-15 in Nevada and from US 93 in Arizona, north of Kingman. Lake Mead Visitor Center is located on Nevada SH 166 (Lakeshore Road) just off US 93. Katherine Ranger Station on Lake Mohave is located on the Katherine Access Road off Arizona SH 68 by Davis Dam. The area includes Lake Mead, located 30 miles southeast of Las Vegas, and Lake Mohave, downstream from Hoover Dam.

Recreation Contact: National Park Service, Lake Mead NRA, 601 Nevada Hwy., Boulder City NV 89005 / 702-293-8990.

Lake Tahoe

BOR Region: Mid-Pacific. Recreation is administered by the U.S. Forest Service, State of California and Nevada. Located in eastern California and western Nevada. The Lake can be accessed from SH 89, off I-80 just west of Truckee, California. The Taylor Creek Visitor Center offers a wide range of maps, brochures, wilderness permits, and interpretive programs about the area. The visitor center is located near Fallen Leaf Lake, in South Lake Tahoe, California off SH 89.

Recreation Contact: Lake Tahoe Basin Management Unit, 870 Emerald Bay Road Suite 1, South Lake Tahoe CA 96150 / 530-583-4379. Lake Tahoe Nevada State Park, 2005 Hwy 28, Incline Village NV 89452

/ 702-831-0494. Emerald Bay State Park, State Route 89, Tahoe City
CA 96142 / 530-525-7277. D.L. Bliss State Park, P.O. Box 266, Tahoma
CA 96142 / 530-525-7232.

Rye Patch Reservoir

BOR Region: Mid-Pacific. Recreation is administered by the State of
Nevada. Located in northwestern Nevada about 32 miles southwest of
Winnemucca. Several access points to the reservoir are available off I-
80. The state recreation area is located south of Humboldt.

Recreation Contact: Rye Patch State Recreation Area, Star Rt. 1,
P.O. Box 215, Lovelock NV 89419 / 702-538-7321.

Primary Game Fish

	Bass	Bluegill	Catfish	Crappie	Pike	Perch	Salmon	Trout	Walleye
1 Davis Dam — Lake Mohave	•				•			•	
2 Hoover Dam									
3 Lahontan Reservoir	•			•	•			•	•
4 Lake Mead NRA	•	•	•	•				•	
5 Lake Tahoe							•	•	
6 Rye Patch Reservoir	•	•	•	•					•

New Mexico

1 Avalon Reservoir
2 Brantley Reservoir
3 Caballo Reservoir
4 El Vado Reservoir
5 Elephant Butte Reservoir

6 Heron Reservoir
7 Lake Sumner
8 Leasburg Diversion Dam
9 Nambe Falls Reservoir
10 Navajo Reservoir

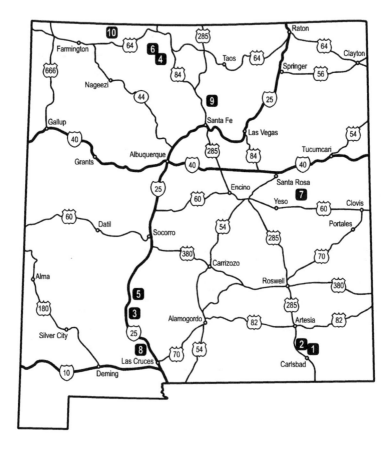

Activities and Facilities

	🏕	🦆	🛶	🎣	🥾	🏊	🪧	⚓	🚻	*i*	♿
1	•	•	•	•	•	•					
2	•	•	•	•	•	•	•		•	•	•
3	•	•	•	•	•	•	•	•	•	•	
4	•	•	•	•	•	•	•		•		•
5	•	•	•	•	•	•	•	•	•	•	
6	•	•	•	•	•	•	•		•	•	•
7	•	•	•	•	•	•	•		•		•
8	•	•	•		•	•	•		•		
9	•	•	•				•		•		
10	•	•	•	•	•	•	•	•	•	•	•

Avalon Reservoir

BOR Region: Upper Colorado. See also Brantley Reservoir. Recreation is administered by Carlsbad Irrigation District. Located in southeastern New Mexico about 4 miles north of Carlsbad. Avalon Reservoir can be reached from Carlsbad by following Canal Street north about 4 miles. The lake is west of Canal Street.

Recreation Contact: Carlsbad Irrigation District, 201 S Canal St., Carlsbad NM 88220 / 505-885-3203.

Brantley Reservoir

BOR Region: Upper Colorado. See also Avalon Reservoir. Recreation is administered by the State of New Mexico. Located in southeastern New Mexico about 12 miles northwest of Carlsbad and 24 miles southeast of Artesia. To reach Brantley Reservoir from Carlsbad, follow US 285 northwest approximately 12 miles. Several local roads off US 285 provide access to the lake.

Recreation Contact: Brantley Lake State Park, P.O. Box 2288, Carlsbad NM 88221 / 505-457-2384.

Caballo Reservoir

BOR Region: Upper Colorado. See also Elephant Butte Reservoir. Recreation is administered by the State of New Mexico. Located in south-central New Mexico, about 20 miles south of Truth or Consequences. The north end of Caballo Reservoir can be reached from Truth or Consequences by traveling south on I-25 to the Las Palomas exit. The southern end of the reservoir is reached from I-25 Exit 59.

Recreation Contact: Caballo Lake State Park, P.O. Box 32, Caballo NM 87931 / 505-743-3942.

El Vado Reservoir

BOR Region: Upper Colorado. See also Heron Reservoir. Recreation is administered by the State of New Mexico. Located in northern New Mexico about 15 miles southwest of Tierra Amarilla. The southern end of the reservoir is reached from US 64/84 near Tierra Amarilla by following SH 112 south about 15 miles. To reach the northern end of the lake, follow SH 95 south from the junction with US 64/84 near Brazos.

Recreation Contact: El Vado Lake State Park, P.O. Box 29, Tierra Amarilla NM 87575 / 505-588-7247.

Elephant Butte Reservoir

BOR Region: Upper Colorado. See also Caballo Reservoir. Recreation is administered by the State of New Mexico. Elephant Butte Reservoir lies east of I-25 and a few miles northeast of Truth or Consequences in south-central New Mexico. Follow SH 51 north out of Truth or Consequences.

Recreation Contact: Elephant Butte Lake State Park, P.O. Box 13, Elephant Butte NM 87935 / 505-744-5421.

Heron Reservoir

BOR Region: Upper Colorado. See also El Vado Reservoir. Recreation is administered by the State of New Mexico. Located in northern

New Mexico about 14 miles southwest of Chama. To reach the reservoir from Chama, follow US 64/84 south to SH 95. Follow SH 95 south about 9 miles to the lake.

Recreation Contact: Heron Lake State Park, P.O. Box 159, Los Ojos NM 87511 / 505-588-7470.

Lake Sumner

BOR Region: Upper Colorado. Recreation is administered by the State of New Mexico. Located in east-central New Mexico, 16 miles northwest of Fort Sumner. The lake is accessed via US 84 north and SH 203 west.

Recreation Contact: Sumner Lake State Park, HC 64 Box 125, Fort Sumner NM 88316 / 505-355-2541.

Leasburg Diversion Dam

BOR Region: Upper Colorado. Recreation is administered by the State of New Mexico. Located in southern New Mexico, about 15 miles north of Las Cruces. The dam can be reached from Las Cruces by traveling north on I-25 for 15 miles to SH 157. Head west on SH 157 to SH 185 and go north to the dam.

Recreation Contact: Leasburg Dam State Park, P.O. Box 6, Radium Springs NM 88054 / 505-524-4068.

Nambe Falls Reservoir

BOR Region: Upper Colorado. Recreation is administered by Nambe Pueblo. Located in northern New Mexico about 18 miles north of Santa Fe. To reach the reservoir from Santa Fe, follow US 84/285 north for 18 miles to SH 503. Follow SH 503 east to Nambe Route 1 and head south to entrance at ranger station.

Recreation Contact: Nambe Pueblo, Rt. 1 Box 117BB, Nambe Pueblo NM 87501 / 505-455-2036.

Navajo Reservoir

BOR Region: Upper Colorado. Recreation is administered by the States of Colorado and New Mexico. Located in southwestern Colorado and northwestern New Mexico, about 45 miles southeast of Durango, Colorado. To reach the state recreation area in Colorado follow SH 151 south off US 160 near Chimney Rock. The recreation areas in New Mexico are accessed from SH 539 and 511 off US 64.

Recreation Contact: New Mexico Recreation Areas: Navajo Lake State Park, 1448 NM 511 #1, Navajo Dam NM 87419 / 505-632-2278. Colorado Recreation Areas: Navajo SRA, P.O. Box 1697, Arboles CO 81121 / 970-883-2208.

Primary Game Fish

	BASS	BLUEGILL	CATFISH	CRAPPIE	PIKE	PERCH	SALMON	TROUT	WALLEYE
1 Avalon Reservoir	•	•	•						
2 Brantley Reservoir	•		•	•					•
3 Caballo Reservoir	•		•	•					•
4 El Vado Reservoir								•	•
5 Elephant Butte Reservoir	•		•	•					•
6 Heron Reservoir								•	•
7 Lake Sumner	•	•	•						•
8 Leasburg Diversion Dam	•		•						
9 Nambe Falls Reservoir								•	•
10 Navajo Reservoir	•		•		•			•	•

North Dakota

1 Brekken-Holmes Recreation Area
2 Devils Lake
3 Edward A. Patterson Lake
4 Jamestown Reservoir
5 Lake Tschida

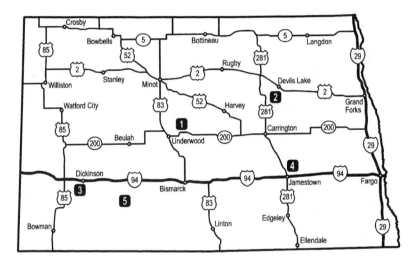

Activities and Facilities

1	•		•		•			•	•		•		
2	•		•	•	•	•	•	•	•		•	
3	•		•	•			•				•	
4	•		•	•	•	•	•	•	•	•	•	
5	•		•	•			•			•	•		•

Brekken-Holmes Recreation Area

BOR Region: Great Plains. Recreation is administered by Turtle Lake Park Board. Located in central North Dakota, near the community of Turtle Lake. Lakes Brekken and Holmes are located just north of the town of Turtle Creek. They can be accessed from SH 41 and CR 27. Turtle Lake is reached from SH 41 near the community of Turtle Lake by following CR 12 west a little over 2 miles.

Recreation Contact: Turtle Lake Park Board, P.O. Box 338, Turtle Lake ND 58575 / 701-448-2596.

Devils Lake

BOR Region: Great Plains. Recreation is administered by the State of North Dakota. Devil's Lake is located in central North Dakota south of the community with the same name. The lake can be accessed from several highways surrounding the lake including: US 2, SH 20, SH 57, and SH 19.

Recreation Contact: North Dakota Parks and Tourism Dept., Rt. 1 Box 165, Devils Lake ND 58301 / 701-662-8418.

Edward A. Patterson Lake

BOR Region: Great Plains. Recreation is administered by Dickinson Park and Recreation District. Located in southwestern North Dakota just south of the community of Dickinson. The northern shore of Patterson Lake is reached from Dickinson by traveling west on Highway 10 from the intersection with Business I-94. The lake's southern shore is accessed from Dickinson by traveling south on SH 22 to 8th Street and heading west.

Recreation Contact: Dickinson Park and Recreation District, Box 548, Dickinson ND 58601 / 701-225-2074.

Jamestown Reservoir

BOR Region: Great Plains. Recreation is administered by Stutsman County Park Board. Located in east-central North Dakota, 2 miles north of Jamestown. Access to the lake is available off US 52/281 and SH 20.

Recreation Contact: Stutsman County Park Board, Jamestown Promotion and Tourism Center, 212 Third Avenue NE, Jamestown ND 58401 / 701-252-4835.

Lake Tschida

BOR Region: Great Plains. Recreation is administered by the Bureau of Reclamation. Located in southern North Dakota between Dickinson and Bismarck. Access is available off SH 49, 15 miles south of Glen Ullin.

Recreation Contact: Bureau of Reclamation, Dakotas Area Office, Box 1017, Bismarck ND 58502 / 701-250-4592.

Primary Game Fish

	Bass	Bluegill	Catfish	Crappie	Pike	Perch	Salmon	Trout	Walleye
1 Brekken-Holmes	•	•		•				•	•
2 Devils Lake				•	•	•			•
3 Edward A. Patterson Lake	•	•		•	•				•
4 Jamestown Reservoir	•	•	•	•	•				•
5 Lake Tschida	•	•	•	•	•	•			•

Oklahoma

1 Altus Lake
2 Arbuckle Lake
3 Fort Cobb Lake
4 Foss Reservoir

5 Lake Thunderbird
6 McGee Creek Reservoir
7 Tom Steed Lake

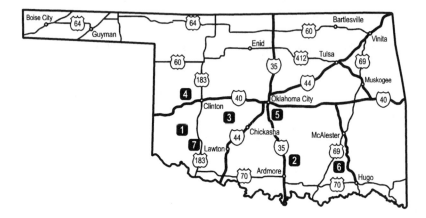

Activities and Facilities

	🏕	🐋	🛶	🏄	🚶	🏊	⛽	⚓	🚻	ℹ	♿
1	•	•	•	•	•	•	•	•	•	•	•
2	•	•	•		•	•			•	•	
3	•	•	•	•	•	•	•	•	•		•
4	•	•	•	•	•	•	•	•	•	•	•
5	•	•	•	•	•	•	•	•	•	•	•
6	•	•	•	•	•	•	•	•	•	•	•
7	•	•	•	•	•	•	•	•	•	•	

Altus Lake

BOR Region: Great Plains. Recreation is administered by the State of Oklahoma. Located in southwestern Oklahoma, about 20 miles north of Altus. From Lone Wolf, the lake can be accessed off SH 44 south or to the west on SH 9.

Recreation Contact: Quartz Mt. State Park, Rt. 1 Box 40, Lone Wolf OK 73655 / 580-563-2238.

Arbuckle Lake

BOR Region: Great Plains. Recreation is administered by the National Park Service. Located in southern Oklahoma, east of I-35, about 28 miles northeast of Ardmore near Sulphur. Access to the lake from Sulphur is available from SH 7 or US 177.

Recreation Contact: Chickasaw National Recreation Area, P.O. Box 201, Sulphur OK 73086 / 580-622-3161.

Fort Cobb Lake

BOR Region: Great Plains. Recreation is administered by the State of Oklahoma. Located in west-central Oklahoma, southwest of Oklahoma City. To reach the lake from Binger on US 281, follow SH 152 west to SH 146. Follow SH 146 south for about 9 miles.

Recreation Contact: Ft. Cobb State Park, P.O. Box 297, Ft. Cobb OK 73038 / 580-643-2249.

Foss Reservoir

BOR Region: Great Plains. Recreation is administered by the State of Oklahoma. Located in western Oklahoma, north of I-40, about 16 miles west of Clinton. From Clinton, follow I-40 west to SH 44, then north to the reservoir.

Recreation Contact: Foss Lake State Park, HC 60 Box 111, Foss OK 73647 / 580-592-4433.

Lake Thunderbird

BOR Region: Great Plains. Recreation is administered by the State of Oklahoma. Located in central Oklahoma, southeast of Oklahoma

City, near Stella. The lake and dam area can be accessed on SH 9.

Recreation Contact: Little River State Park, Rt 4 Box 277, Norman OK 73071 / 405-364-7634.

McGee Creek Reservoir

BOR Region: Great Plains. Recreation is administered by the State of Oklahoma. Located in southeastern Oklahoma about 40 miles south of McAlester. To reach the reservoir from McAlester, travel south on US 69 to Atoka. From Atoka, follow SH 3 east for 13 miles.

Recreation Contact: McGee Creek State Park, Rt 1 Box 6A, Farris OK 74542 / 580-364-7634.

Tom Steed Lake

BOR Region: Great Plains. Recreation is administered by the State of Oklahoma. Located in southwestern Oklahoma, northeast of Altus near Mountain Park. Access to the park and lake is off US 183 a couple miles north of Mountain Park.

Recreation Contact: Great Plains State Park, Rt1 Box 52, Mountain Park OK 73559 / 580-569-2032.

Primary Game Fish

		BASS	BLUEGILL	CATFISH	CRAPPIE	PIKE	PERCH	SALMON	TROUT	WALLEYE
1	Altus Lake	•			•	•				•
2	Arbuckle Lake	•	•		•	•				
3	Fort Cobb Lake	•			•	•				
4	Foss Reservoir	•			•	•				
5	Lake Thunderbird	•			•	•				
6	McGee Creek Reservoir	•	•		•	•				
7	Tom Steed Lake	•				•				•

OREGON

1	Agate Reservoir	12	Howard Prairie Lake
2	Beulah Reservoir	13	Hyatt Reservoir
3	Bully Creek Reservoir	14	McKay Reservoir
4	Clear Lake	15	Ochoco Reservoir
5	Cold Springs Reservoir	16	Owyhee Reservoir
6	Crane Prairie Reservoir	17	Phillips Lake
7	Crescent Lake	18	Prineville Reservoir
8	Emigrant Lake	19	Thief Valley Reservoir
9	Gerber Reservoir	20	Unity Reservoir
10	Haystack Reservoir	21	Warm Springs Reservoir
11	Henry Hagg Lake	22	Wickiup Reservoir

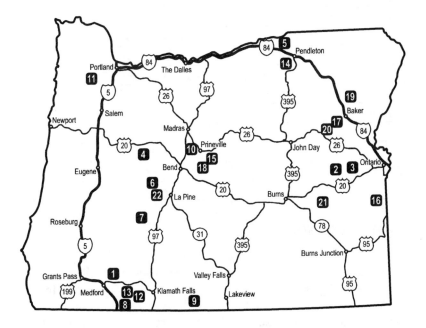

Activities and Facilities

	🏕	🚤	🛶	🎣	🥾	🏊	⛱	⚓	🚻	ℹ	♿
1		•	•	•		•	•			•	
2	•	•	•	•			•			•	
3	•	•	•	•		•	•			•	
4	•	•	•	•	•	•				•	
5		•	•	•							
6	•	•	•	•					•	•	
7	•	•	•			•	•		•	•	
8	•	•	•	•	•	•	•			•	
9	•	•	•		•		•			•	
10	•	•	•	•		•	•			•	•
11		•	•		•	•	•			•	•
12	•	•	•	•	•	•	•		•	•	
13	•	•	•	•		•	•			•	
14		•	•	•		•	•			•	
15	•	•	•	•		•	•			•	
16	•	•	•	•		•	•		•	•	
17	•	•	•	•		•	•			•	
18	•	•	•	•		•	•		•	•	
19	•	•	•	•		•	•			•	
20	•	•	•	•			•			•	
21		•	•	•		•				•	
22	•	•	•	•		•	•		•	•	

Agate Reservoir

BOR Region: Pacific Northwest. Recreation is administered by Jackson County. Located in southwestern Oregon about 10 miles northeast of Medford. Agate Reservoir can be reached from Medford by following SH 62 north to SH 140. Follow SH 140 east about 4 miles.

Recreation Contact: Jackson County Parks and Recreation Dept., 10 S Oakdale, County Courthouse, Medford OR 97501 / 541-776-7001.

Beulah Reservoir

BOR Region: Pacific Northwest. Recreation is administered by Malheur County. Located in eastern Oregon about 70 miles northeast of Burns. The reservoir is accessed off US 20 in Juntura, travel north on Beulah Road for 14 miles.

Recreation Contact: Malheur County, Beulah Reservoir, 251 B St. West, Vale OR 97918 / 541-473-5191.

Bully Creek Reservoir

BOR Region: Pacific Northwest. Recreation is administered by Malheur County. Located in eastern Oregon about 25 miles west of Ontario. The reservoir is reached 10 miles west of Vale off Graham Blvd. Paved access to the dam.

Recreation Contact: Malheur County, Bully Creek Reservoir, 251 B St. West, Vale OR 97918 / 541-473-5191.

Clear Lake

BOR Region: Pacific Northwest. Recreation is administered by the U.S. Forest Service. Located in west-central Oregon in the Cascade Mountains. From Sweet Home travel 55 miles east on US 20, then south on SH 126.

Recreation Contact: Willamette National Forest, 2955 NW Division St., Gresham OR 97030 / 541-465-6521.

Cold Springs Reservoir

BOR Region: Pacific Northwest. Recreation is administered by the U.S. Fish and Wildlife Service. Located in northern Oregon, near the Washington border, north of I-84. To reach the area from Hermiston travel about 7 miles east on SH 207.

Recreation Contact: U.S. Fish and Wildlife Service, Cold Springs NWR, P.O. Box 239, Umatilla OR 97882 / 541-922-3232.

Crane Prairie Reservoir

BOR Region: Pacific Northwest. See also Wickiup Reservoir. Recreation is administered by the U.S. Forest Service. Located in central

Oregon in the Cascade Mountains about 40 miles southwest of Bend. The reservoir can be reached off US 97, north of La Pine, by traveling west on CR 43 and CR 42 for 20 miles to Odell Road. Follow Odell Road north one mile to the reservoir.

Recreation Contact: Deschutes National Forest, 1625 Hwy. 20 East, Bend OR 97701 / 541-388-2715.

Crescent Lake

BOR Region: Pacific Northwest. Recreation is administered by the U.S. Forest Service. Located in central Oregon about 33 miles southeast of Oakridge. To reach the lake from Oakridge, follow SH 58 southeast for 33 miles to Crescent Lake Junction. Follow Crescent Lake Highway southwest for a couple of miles.

Recreation Contact: Deschutes National Forest, 1625 Hwy. 20 East, Bend OR 97701 / 541-388-2715.

Emigrant Lake

BOR Region: Pacific Northwest. Recreation is administered by Jackson County. Located in southwestern Oregon about 5 miles southeast of Ashland. Follow SH 66 southeast out of Ashland to reach the lake. Vehicle access is good along the west arm and limited on east arm.

Recreation Contact: Jackson County Parks, Emigrant Lake, 400 Antelope Rd., White City OR 97501 / 541-776-7001.

Gerber Reservoir

BOR Region: Mid-Pacific. Recreation is administered by the Bureau of Land Management. Located in southern Oregon, about 45 miles east of Klamath Falls. The reservoir can be reached from SH 70 in Bonanza by following Langell Valley and Gerber Roads east for 19 miles.

Recreation Contact: Bureau of Land Management, Klamath Falls Resource Area, 2795 Anderson Avenue, Building 25, Klamath Falls OR 97603 / 541-883-6916.

Haystack Reservoir

BOR Region: Pacific Northwest. Recreation is administered by the Forest Service. Haystack Reservoir is located in the Crooked River

National Grassland in central Oregon. The lake is reached from Madras by following US 97 south to Jerico Lane. Follow Jerico Lane southeast to the reservoir.

Recreation Contact: Deschutes National Forest, 1625 Hwy. 20 East, Bend OR 97701 / 541-388-2715.

Henry Hagg Lake

BOR Region: Pacific Northwest. Recreation is administered by Washington County. Located in northwestern Oregon about 30 miles west of Portland. From Forest Grove, follow SH 47 south to Scoggins Valley Road and travel west about 2 miles.

Recreation Contact: Washington County, Henry Hagg Lake, 150 N First Ave., Hillsboro OR 97124 / 503-359-5732.

Howard Prairie Lake

BOR Region: Pacific Northwest. See also Hyatt Reservoir. Recreation is administered by Jackson County. Located in southwestern Oregon about 15 miles east of Ashland. From SH 66 near Ashland, follow Dead Indian Road northeast to Hyatt Prairie Road, then south to the lake.

Recreation Contact: Jackson County Parks, Howard Prairie Lake, 400 Antelope Rd., White City OR 97501 / 541-776-7001.

Hyatt Reservoir

BOR Region: Pacific Northwest. See also Howard Prairie Lake. Recreation is administered by the Bureau of Land Management. Located in southwestern Oregon about 15 miles east of Ashland. Hyatt Reservoir is southwest of Howard Prairie Lake. From SH 66 near Ashton, follow Dead Indian Road northeast to Hyatt Prairie Road, then south to the lake.

Recreation Contact: Bureau of Land Management, 3040 Biddle Rd., Medford OR 97501 / 541-770-2200.

McKay Reservoir

BOR Region: Pacific Northwest. Recreation is administered by the U.S. Fish and Wildlife Service. Located in northeastern Oregon 8 miles south of Pendleton. To reach the reservoir from Pendleton, follow US

395 south about 4 miles. The lake lies east of US 395.

Recreation Contact: U.S. Fish and Wildlife, McKay Creek National Wildlife Refuge, P.O. Box 239, Umatilla OR 97882 / 541-922-3232.

Ochoco Reservoir

BOR Region: Pacific Northwest. See also Prineville Reservoir. Recreation is administered by the State of Oregon. Located in central Oregon about 5 miles east of Prineville off US 26.

Recreation Contact: Ochoco Lake State Park, 91677 Parkland Dr., Prineville OR 97754 / 541-447-4363.

Owyhee Reservoir

BOR Region: Pacific Northwest. Recreation is administered by the State of Oregon. Located in eastern Oregon about 50 miles south of Ontario. Follow SH 201 south from Ontario to Owyhee Avenue north of Adrian. Other local roads heading west from SH 201 provide access to the lake's eastern shore.

Recreation Contact: Oregon Parks and Recreation Dept., Lake Owyhee State Park, 2034 Auburn, Baker City OR 97814 / 541-523-2499.

Phillips Lake

BOR Region: Pacific Northwest. Recreation is administered by the U.S. Forest Service. Located in eastern Oregon about 15 miles southwest of Baker City. The lake is accessible from SH 7.

Recreation Contact: Wallowa-Whitman National Forest, Baker Ranger District, 3165 10th St., Baker City OR 97814 / 541-523-4476.

Prineville Reservoir

BOR Region: Pacific Northwest. See also Ochoco Reservoir. Recreation is administered by the State of Oregon. Located in central Oregon about 15 miles south of Prineville. Good access to north side of reservoir via Juniper Canyon Rd. South side and lower end of reservoir access via scenic drive up the Crooked River and over Bowman Dam.

Turn off US 26 in town of Prineville to reach both routes.

Recreation Contact: Prineville Reservoir State Park, PLR Box 1050, Prineville OR 97754 / 541-447-4363.

Thief Valley Reservoir

BOR Region: Pacific Northwest. Recreation is administered by Union County. Located in northeastern Oregon about 25 miles north of Baker City. To reach the lake from Baker City, travel north on I-84 to SH 203. Follow SH 203 northeast to Telocaset Lane north of Pondosa. Follow Telocaset Lane northwest to the lake's entrance road.

Recreation Contact: Union County, Union County Courthouse, 1106 K Ave., La Grande OR 97850 / 541-963-1001.

Unity Reservoir

BOR Region: Pacific Northwest. Recreation is administered by the State of Oregon. Located in eastern Oregon about 5 miles north of the community of Unity. To reach the lake from Unity, travel north on US 26 for 2 miles to SH 245. Follow SH 245 north to the reservoir.

Recreation Contact: Unity Lake State Park, P.O. Box 850, La Grande OR 97850 / 541-963-6444.

Warm Springs Reservoir

BOR Region: Pacific Northwest. Recreation is administered by the Bureau of Reclamation. Located in eastern Oregon approximately 55 miles east of Burns. To reach the lake from Juntura, follow the Juntura-Riverside Road south for 12 miles. Travel west about 2 miles on lake access roads. Access is via a narrow, winding, gravel road.

Recreation Contact: Bureau of Reclamation, Snake River Area Office, 214 Broadway Avenue, Boise ID 83702 / 208-334-1460.

Wickiup Reservoir

BOR Region: Pacific Northwest. See also Crane Prairie Reservoir. Recreation is administered by the U.S. Forest Service. Located in central Oregon in the Cascade Mountains about 40 miles southwest of Bend. The reservoir can be reached off US 97, north of La Pine, by traveling

west on CR 43 to Wickiup Road. Follow Wickiup Road south to the
reservoir.

Recreation Contact: Deschutes National Forest, 1645 Hwy. 20 East,
Bend OR 97701 / 541-388-2715.

Primary Game Fish

	Bass	Bluegill	Catfish	Crappie	Pike	Perch	Salmon	Trout	Walleye
1 Agate Reservoir	•	•	•	•		•		•	
2 Beulah Reservoir								•	
3 Bully Creek Reservoir	•			•				•	
4 Clear Lake								•	
5 Cold Springs Reservoir	•			•	•				
6 Crane Prairie Reservoir	•							•	•
7 Crescent Lake								•	•
8 Emigrant Lake	•			•	•			•	•
9 Gerber Reservoir	•			•				•	
10 Haystack Reservoir	•			•	•			•	•
11 Henry Hagg Lake	•			•			•	•	
12 Howard Prairie Lake	•			•				•	
13 Hyatt Reservoir	•							•	
14 McKay Reservoir	•	•			•		•	•	
15 Ochoco Reservoir				•				•	
16 Owyhee Reservoir	•			•	•		•	•	
17 Phillips Lake	•				•		•	•	•
18 Prineville Reservoir	•			•	•			•	
19 Thief Valley Reservoir					•			•	
20 Unity Reservoir	•				•			•	
21 Warm Springs Reservoir	•	•	•					•	
22 Wickiup Reservoir								•	•

SOUTH DAKOTA

1	Angostura Reservoir	4	Lake Byron
2	Belle Fourche Reservoir	5	Pactola Reservoir
3	Deerfield Reservoir	6	Shadehill Reservoir

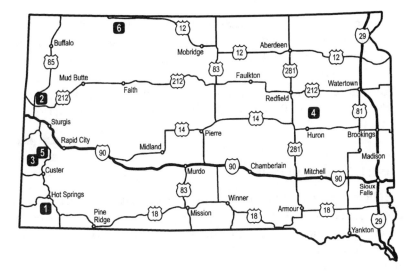

Activities and Facilities

	🏕	🐋	🚣	🎣	🚶	🏊	🏕	⚓	🚻	*i*	♿
1	•	•	•	•	•	•	•	•	•	•	•
2	•	•	•	•		•			•		
3	•	•	•	•	•	•	•	•	•		
4		•	•	•		•	•		•		
5	•	•	•	•	•	•	•	•	•	•	
6	•	•	•	•	•	•	•		•		

Angostura Reservoir

BOR Region: Great Plains. Recreation is administered by the State of South Dakota. Located in southwestern South Dakota about 9 miles south of Hot Springs off US 18/385.

Recreation Contact: Angostura SRA, P.O. Box 131-A, Hot Springs SD 57747 / 605-745-6996.

Belle Fourche Reservoir

BOR Region: Great Plains. Recreation is administered by the State of South Dakota. Located in western South Dakota, north of Spearfish, about 8 miles east of Belle Fourche. The reservoir is accessed north of US 212 from Belle Fourche.

Recreation Contact: South Dakota Department of Game, Fish and Parks, Belle Fourche Reservoir, 3305 W South St., Rapid City SD 57702 / 605-394-2391.

Deerfield Reservoir

BOR Region: Great Plains. See also Pactola Reservoir. Recreation is administered by the U.S. Forest Service. Deerfield Reservoir is in the Black Hills National Forest 25 miles west of Rapid City. To reach the reservoir from US 16 near Hill City, follow Deerfield Road northwest about 14 miles.

Recreation Contact: Black Hills National Forest, Harney Ranger District, 23939 Hwy 385, Hill City SD 57745 / 605-574-2534.

Lake Byron

BOR Region: Great Plains. Recreation is administered by the State of South Dakota. Located in east-central South Dakota about 17 miles north of Huron. To reach the lake from Huron, follow SH 37 north 14 miles to CR 8, then east for 3 miles.

Recreation Contact: South Dakota Department of Game, Fish and Parks, Lake Byron, 895 3rd St SW, Huron SD 57350 / 605-353-7145.

Pactola Reservoir

BOR Region: Great Plains. See also Deerfield Reservoir. Recreation is administered by the U.S Forest Service. Located in western South Dakota about 19 miles west of Rapid City. From Rapid City follow SH 44 west for 17 miles to US 385. Follow US 385 south 2 miles to the reservoir.

Recreation Contact: Black Hills National Forest, 803 Soo San Dr., Rapid City SD 57702 / 605-343-1567.

Shadehill Reservoir

BOR Region: Great Plains. Recreation is administered by the State of South Dakota. Located in northwestern South Dakota near the North Dakota border, 12 miles south of Lemmon. To reach the reservoir from US 12 near Lemmon, follow SH 73 south about 11 miles to CR 2. Follow CR 2 west to the reservoir.

Recreation Contact: Shadehill SRA, P.O. Box 63, Shadehill SD 57653 / 605-374-5114.

Primary Game Fish

	Bass	Bluegill	Catfish	Crappie	Pike	Perch	Salmon	Trout	Walleye
1 Angostura Reservoir	•			•					•
2 Belle Fourche Reservoir	•		•						•
3 Deerfield Reservoir	•							•	
4 Lake Byron				•	•				•
5 Pactola Reservoir							•	•	
6 Shadehill Reservoir	•		•						•

TEXAS

1 Choke Canyon Reservoir
2 Lake Meredith NRA
3 Lake Texana
4 Twin Buttes Reservoir

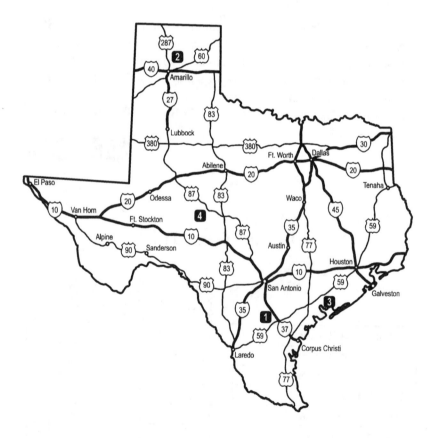

Activities and Facilities

🏕	🚤	🛶	🎣	🚶	🏊	🏕	⚓	🚻	*i*	♿
1	•	•	•	•	•	•	•		•	•	•
2	•	•	•	•	•	•	•	•	•	•	•
3	•	•	•		•	•	•		•	•	•
4	•	•	•	•	•	•	•	•	•		

Choke Canyon Reservoir

BOR Region: Great Plains. Recreation is administered by the State of Texas. Located in southern Texas, just west of I-37, south of San Antonio. The reservoir can be accessed from numerous roads including County Road 99, north of Three Rivers, off either I-37 or US Alt 281.

Recreation Contact: Choke Canyon State Park, Calliham Unit, P.O. Box 2, Calliham TX 78007 / 512-786-3868. Choke Canyon State Park, Choke Canyon South Shore, P.O. Box 1548, Three Rivers TX 78071 / 512-786-3538. Daughtrey Wildlife Management Area, P.O. Box 388, George West TX 78022 / 512-358-2124.

Lake Meredith National Recreation Area

BOR Region: Great Plains. Recreation is administered by the National Park Service. Located north of I-40 and Amarillo in northwest Texas. The recreation areas can be accessed from several routes around the lake including SH 136 north out of Amarillo.

Recreation Contact: National Park service, Lake Meredith NRA, P.O. Box 1460, Fritch TX 79036 / 806-857-2002.

Lake Texana

BOR Region: Great Plains. Recreation is administered by the State of Texas. Located in southeastern Texas, northeast of Victoria, near

Edna. From Edna the lake can be accessed from either US 59 or SH 111.

Recreation Contact: Lake Texana State Park, P.O. Box 760, Edna TX 77957 / 512-782-5718.

Twin Buttes Reservoir

BOR Region: Great Plains. Recreation is administered by San Angelo Water Supply Corp. Located in central Texas about 15 miles south of San Angelo. From San Angelo the reservoir can be reached from either US 67 or US 277.

Recreation Contact: San Angelo Water Supply Corp., Twin Buttes Reservoir, P.O. Box 1630, San Angelo TX 76902 / 915-655-9140.

Primary Game Fish

	Bass	Bluegill	Catfish	Crappie	Pike	Perch	Salmon	Trout	Walleye
1 Choke Canyon Reservoir	•		•	•					
2 Lake Meredith NRA	•		•	•					•
3 Lake Texana	•		•	•					•
4 Twin Buttes Reservoir	•	•	•	•		•			

UTAH

1 Causey Reservoir
2 Currant Creek Reservoir
3 Deer Creek Reservoir
4 East Canyon Reservoir
5 Echo Reservoir
6 Flaming Gorge NRA
7 Huntington North Reservoir
8 Hyrum Reservoir
9 Joes Valley Reservoir
10 Jordanelle Reservoir

11 Lake Powell,
   Glen Canyon NRA
12 Lost Creek Reservoir
13 Meeks Cabin Reservoir
14 Moon Lake Reservoir
15 Newton Reservoir
16 Pineview Reservoir
17 Red Fleet Reservoir
18 Rockport Reservoir
19 Scofield Reservoir
20 Starvation Reservoir
21 Stateline Reservoir
22 Steinaker Reservoir
23 Strawberry Reservoir
24 Upper Stillwater Reservoir
25 Willard Reservoir

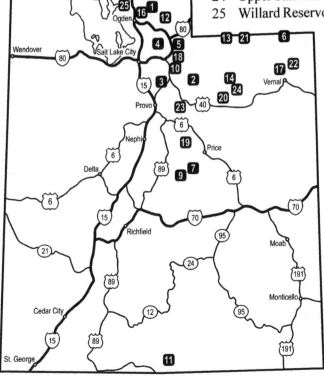

Activities and Facilities

#	🏕	🦭	🛶	🚡	🚶	🏊	⛱	⚓	🚻	i	♿
1		•	•	•	•	•	•		•		
2	•	•	•	•	•	•	•		•		•
3	•	•	•	•		•	•	•	•		•
4	•	•	•	•	•	•	•		•		•
5	•	•	•			•	•		•		
6	•	•	•	•	•	•	•	•	•	•	•
7	•	•	•	•		•	•		•		•
8	•	•	•	•		•	•		•		•
9	•	•	•	•	•		•	•	•		•
10	•	•	•		•	•	•	•	•	•	•
11	•	•	•	•	•	•	•	•	•	•	•
12	•	•	•	•		•			•		
13	•	•	•	•	•	•	•		•		
14	•	•	•	•	•	•	•		•		
15	•	•	•	•		•	•		•		
16	•	•	•	•	•	•	•	•	•		•
17	•	•	•	•		•	•		•		
18	•	•	•	•		•	•		•		•
19	•	•	•	•	•		•		•		•
20	•	•	•	•		•	•		•		•
21	•	•	•	•	•	•	•		•		•
22	•	•	•	•		•	•		•		•
23	•	•	•	•	•	•	•	•	•	•	•
24	•	•	•	•	•		•		•		•
25	•	•	•	•		•	•	•	•		•

Causey Reservoir

BOR Region: Upper Colorado. See also Lost Creek and Pineview Reservoirs. Recreation is administered by the U.S. Forest Service. Located in northern Utah about 20 miles northeast of Ogden. From Ogden, follow SH 39 east for 19 miles to Causey Drive.

Recreation Contact: Wasatch-Cache National Forest, Ogden Ranger District, 507 25th Street Suite 103, Ogden UT 84402 / 801-625-5112.

Currant Creek Reservoir

BOR Region: Upper Colorado. See also Starvation Reservoir. Recreation is administered by the U.S. Forest Service. Located 40 miles southeast of Heber City. To reach the reservoir from US 40 near Fruitland, follow Current Creek Road north about 16 miles.

Recreation Contact: Uinta National Forest, Heber Ranger District, P.O. Box 190, Heber City UT 84032 / 435-654-0470.

Deer Creek Reservoir

BOR Region: Upper Colorado. See also Jordanelle Reservoir. Recreation is administered by the State of Utah. Located in north-central Utah about 7 miles southwest of Heber City. The reservoir can be accessed from US 189 out of Heber City.

Recreation Contact: Deer Creek State Park, P.O. Box 257, Midway UT 84049 / 435-654-0171.

East Canyon Reservoir

BOR Region: Upper Colorado. See also Echo and Rockport Reservoirs. Recreation is administered by the State of Utah. Located in northern Utah 12 miles south of Morgan. The reservoir can be accessed from SH 65 and SH 66, both off I-84.

Recreation Contact: East Canyon State Park, P.O. Box 97, Morgan UT 84050 / 435-829-6866.

Echo Reservoir

BOR Region: Upper Colorado. See also East Canyon and Rockport Reservoirs. Recreation is administered by Echo Resort Inc. Located in northern Utah, north of Coalville. The lake can be accessed from I-84 near the town of Echo.

Recreation Contact: Echo Resort Inc., P.O. Box 746, Coalville UT 84017 / 801-336-2247.

Flaming Gorge NRA

BOR Region: Upper Colorado. Recreation is administered by the U.S. Forest Service. Located in northeastern Utah and southwestern Wyoming. From Vernal, Utah follow US 191 north 20 miles. Access is provided along US 191 and SH 44 in Utah, and US 191 and SH 530 in Wyoming.

Recreation Contact: Ashley National Forest, Flaming Gorge NRA, P.O. Box 279, Manila UT 84046 / 435-784-3445.

Huntington North Reservoir

BOR Region: Upper Colorado. See also Joes Valley Reservoir. Recreation is administered by the State of Utah. The reservoir is located in central Utah about 20 miles south of Price. To reach the lake from Price, follow SH 10 south.

Recreation Contact: Huntington State Park, P.O. Box 1343, Huntington UT 84528 / 435-687-2491.

Hyrum Reservoir

BOR Region: Upper Colorado. See also Willard Reservoir. Recreation is administered by the State of Utah. Located in northern Utah south of Logan. The reservoir is reached from Logan by following SH 165 south for 6 miles.

Recreation Contact: Hyrum State Park, 405 West 300 South, Hyrum UT 84319 / 435-245-6866.

Joes Valley Reservoir

BOR Region: Upper Colorado. See also Huntington North Reservoir. Recreation is administered by the U.S. Forest Service. Located in central Utah about 20 miles east of Ephraim. The reservoir is accessed along SH 29 from either Orangeville off SH 10 or Ephraim off US 89.

Recreation Contact: Manti-LaSal National Forest, Ferron Ranger District, P.O. Box 310, Ferron UT 84523 / 435-384-2372.

Jordanelle Reservoir

BOR Region: Upper Colorado. See also Deer Creek and Rockport Reservoirs. Recreation is administered by the State of Utah. Located 10 miles north of Heber City. All-weather access from US 40 or SH 32 from Francis, Kamas, Heber City and Park City East.

Recreation Contact: Jordanelle State Park, P.O. Box 309, Heber City UT 84032 / 435-783-3030 Rock Cliff Unit, and 435-649-9540 Hailstone Unit.

Lake Powell — Glen Canyon NRA

BOR Region: Upper Colorado. Recreation is administered by the National Park Service. Located in northern Arizona and southern Utah, just outside of Page, Arizona. The area is accessed off US 89 from either state.

Recreation Contact: National Park Service, Glen Canyon NRA, P.O. Box 1507, Page AZ 86040 / 520-608-6404 general information, 520-608-6200 headquarters.

Lost Creek Reservoir

BOR Region: Upper Colorado. See also Causey Reservoir. Recreation is administered by the State of Utah. Located in northern Utah east of Ogden. From I-84 near Croydon travel north on Lost Creek Road about 12 miles to the reservoir. All-weather access to dam. Improved gravel roads beyond.

Recreation Contact: Lost Creek State Park, P.O. Box 97, Morgan UT 84050 / 435-829-6866.

Meeks Cabin Reservoir

BOR Region: Upper Colorado. See also Stateline Reservoir. Recreation is administered by the U.S. Forest Service. Located in northern Utah and southwest Wyoming. The lake is reached from Mountain View,

Wyoming by traveling south on SH 410 for 13 miles to CR 271. Follow CR 271 south for 15 miles to the reservoir.

Recreation Contact: Wasatch-Cache National Forest, Evanston Ranger District, 1565 Hwy 150 S., P.O. Box 1880, Evanston WY 82930 / 307-789-3194.

Moon Lake Reservoir

BOR Region: Upper Colorado. Recreation is administered by the U.S. Forest Service. Located in northeastern Utah about 15 miles north of Mountain Home. Access requires high clearance vehicles across the Indian Reservation to Forest Service Road 134.

Recreation Contact: Ashley National Forest, Roosevelt District Ranger, P.O. Box 333-6, Roosevelt UT 84066 / 435-722-5018.

Newton Reservoir

BOR Region: Upper Colorado. Recreation is administered by the Bureau of Reclamation. Located in northern Utah near the Idaho border, east of I-15. To reach the reservoir from Richmond on US 91, travel west for 9 miles on SH 142. The reservoir lies south of SH 142.

Recreation Contact: Bureau of Reclamation, Provo Projects Office, 302 E 1860 S, Provo UT 84606 / 801-379-1000.

Pineview Reservoir

BOR Region: Upper Colorado. See also Causey Reservoir. Recreation is administered by the U.S. Forest Service. Located in northern Utah about 10 miles east of Ogden. To reach the reservoir from Ogden, follow SH 39 east.

Recreation Contact: Wasatch-Cache National Forest, Ogden Ranger District, 507 25th St. Suite 103, Ogden UT 84402 / 801-625-5112.

Red Fleet Reservoir

BOR Region: Upper Colorado. See also Steinaker Reservoir. Recreation is administered by the State of Utah. Located in northeastern Utah north of Vernal. From Vernal follow US 191 north approximately 10 miles. The reservoir is just east of US 191.

Recreation Contact: Red Fleet State Park, 8750 N US 191, Vernal UT 84078 / 435-789-4432.

Rockport Reservoir

BOR Region: Upper Colorado. See also East Canyon, Echo, and Jordanelle Reservoirs. Recreation is administered by the State of Utah. Located in northern Utah, east of Salt Lake City, 5 miles south of Wanship. The reservoir is accessed from SH 32.

Recreation Contact: Rockport State Park, 9040 South State 303, Rockport UT 84036 / 435-336-2241.

Scofield Reservoir

BOR Region: Upper Colorado. Recreation is administered by the State of Utah. Located in central Utah, northwest of Helper, about 3 miles north of the community of Scofield. The reservoir is accessed from SH 96 off US 6 near Colton.

Recreation Contact: Scofield State Park, P.O. Box 166, Price UT 84501 / 435-448-9449 (summer), 435-637-8497 (winter).

Starvation Reservoir

BOR Region: Upper Colorado. See also Currant Creek Reservoir. Recreation is administered by the State of Utah. Located in eastern Utah about 30 miles west of Roosevelt. The lake lies north of US 40 a few miles west of Duchesne.

Recreation Contact: Starvation State Park, P.O. Box 584, Duchesne UT 84021 / 435-738-2326.

Stateline Reservoir

BOR Region: Upper Colorado. See also Meeks Cabin Reservoir. Recreation is administered by the U.S. Forest Service. Located in northern Utah and southwest Wyoming about 20 miles south of Mountain View, Wyoming. Follow SH 410 south for about 7 miles from Mountain View.

Follow CR 246 south for 8 miles to the national forest boundary and then south on FSR 72 for 5 miles. Forest Service Road 72 is an improved gravel road.

Recreation Contact: Wasatch-Cache National Forest, Mountain View Ranger District, P.O. Box 129, Mountain View WY 82939 / 307-782-6555.

Steinaker Reservoir

BOR Region: Upper Colorado. See also Red Fleet Reservoir. Recreation is administered by the State of Utah. Located in northeastern Utah about 7 miles north of Vernal. The reservoir is accessed off US 191.

Recreation Contact: Steinaker State Park, 4335 N US 191, Vernal UT 84078 / 435-789-4432.

Strawberry Reservoir

BOR Region: Upper Colorado. Recreation is administered by the U.S. Forest Service. Located in central Utah about 25 miles southeast of Heber City. To reach the reservoir from Heber City, follow US 40 southeast.

Recreation Contact: Uinta National Forest, Heber Ranger District, P.O. Box 190, Heber City UT 84032 / 435-654-0470.

Upper Stillwater Reservoir

BOR Region: Upper Colorado. Recreation is administered by the U.S. Forest Service. Located in northeastern Utah about 10 miles northwest of Mountain Home. Access is over improved gravel Forest Service Rd. 134.

Recreation Contact: Ashley National Forest, Duchesne Ranger District, P.O. Box 1, Duchesne UT 84026 / 435-738-2482.

Willard Reservoir

BOR Region: Upper Colorado. See also Hyrum Reservoir. Recreation is administered by the State of Utah. Located in northern Utah about 10 miles north of Ogden off I-84.

Recreation Contact: Willard Bay State Park, 650 North 900 West #A, Willard UT 84340 / 801-734-9494.

Primary Game Fish

	BASS	BLUEGILL	CATFISH	CRAPPIE	PIKE	PERCH	SALMON	TROUT	WALLEYE
1 Causey Reservoir								•	
2 Currant Creek Reservoir								•	
3 Deer Creek Reservoir	•							•	
4 East Canyon Reservoir								•	
5 Echo Reservoir				•				•	
6 Flaming Gorge NRA	•						•	•	
7 Huntington North Res.	•	•						•	
8 Hyrum Reservoir			•				•	•	
9 Joes Valley Reservoir								•	
10 Jordanelle Reservoir	•							•	
11 Lake Powell	•			•	•	•		•	•
12 Lost Creek Reservoir								•	
13 Meeks Cabin Reservoir								•	
14 Moon Lake Reservoir								•	
15 Newton Reservoir		•					•	•	
16 Pineview Reservoir		•		•	•				
17 Red Fleet Reservoir	•	•						•	
18 Rockport Reservoir	•							•	
19 Scofield Reservoir								•	
20 Starvation Reservoir	•							•	•
21 Stateline Reservoir								•	
22 Steinaker Reservoir	•							•	
23 Strawberry Reservoir								•	
24 Upper Stillwater Res.								•	
25 Willard Reservoir				•	•				•

WASHINGTON

1 Banks Lake
2 Billy Clapp Lake
3 Bumping Lake
4 Cle Elum Lake
5 Columbia Basin HMA
6 Columbia NWR
7 Conconully Lake
8 Desert Wildlife
     Recreation Area
9 Easton Diversion Dam

10 Franklin D Roosevelt Lake,
     Coulee Dam NRA
11 Kachess Lake
12 Keechelus Lake
13 Potholes Reservoir
14 Quincy Lakes
15 Rimrock and Clear Lakes
16 Roza Diversion Dam
17 Scooteney Reservoir
18 Spectacle Lake

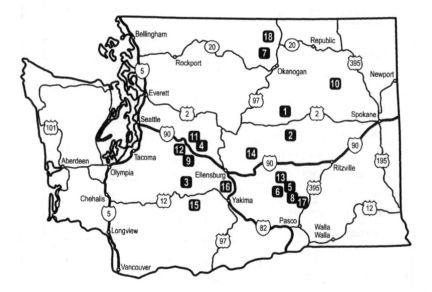

Activities and Facilities

	🏕	🦭	🛶	🎣	🥾	🏊	🪑	⚓	🚻	ℹ️	♿
1	•	•	•	•		•	•	•	•		
2		•	•	•		•	•		•		
3	•	•	•	•		•	•	•	•		
4	•	•	•	•		•	•		•		
5	•	•	•	•	•		•		•		
6		•	•	•	•	•	•		•		
7	•	•	•	•		•	•		•		
8	•	•	•	•		•			•		
9	•	•	•			•	•		•		
10	•	•	•	•	•	•	•	•	•	•	•
11	•	•	•	•		•	•		•		
12		•	•	•		•	•		•		
13	•	•	•	•		•	•	•	•		
14	•	•	•	•		•	•		•		
15	•	•	•	•		•	•	•	•		
16		•	•	•		•			•		
17	•	•	•	•		•	•		•		•
18		•	•	•		•	•	•	•		

Banks Lake

BOR Region: Pacific Northwest. See also Billy Clapp Lake. Recreation is administered by the State of Washington. Located in east-central Washington, northeast of Ephrata, near Coulee City. Access is provided at several locations along SH 155, north of Coulee City.

Recreation Contact: Washington Department of Wildlife, 1540 Alder St. NW, Ephrata WA 98823 / 509-754-4624. Washington State Parks, Steamboat Rock State Park, 2201 N Duncan Dr., Wenatchee WA 98801 / 509-662-0420.

Billy Clapp Lake

BOR Region: Pacific Northwest. See also Banks Lake. Recreation is administered by the State of Washington. Located in east-central Washington about 20 miles northeast of Ephrata, near Stratford. The lake is accessed off SH 28, east of Soap Lake or from Coulee City by traveling south on Pinto Ridge Road. Lands around the lake are included in a wildlife reserve program. Access is limited. Summer Falls State Park is on the north end of lake.

Recreation Contact: Washington Department of Wildlife, 1540 Alder St. NW, Ephrata WA 98823 / 509-754-4624. Summer Falls State Park, Box 136, Coulee City WA 99115.

Bumping Lake

BOR Region: Pacific Northwest. Recreation is administered by the U.S. Forest Service. Located in south-central Washington, east of Mount Rainier National Park in the Cascade Mountains. The lake is accessed off SH 410, west of Cliffdell, by traveling south on Bumping Lake Road.

Recreation Contact: Snoqualmie National Forest, 10061 Hwy. 12, Naches WA 98937 / 509-653-2205.

Cle Elum Lake

BOR Region: Pacific Northwest. See also Kachess Lake and Easton Diversion Dam. Recreation is administered by the U.S. Forest Service. Located in central Washington about 30 miles northwest of Ellensburg, north of I-90. The lake is accessed from SH 903, off I-90, just west of the community of Cle Elum.

Recreation Contact: Wenatchee National Forest, P.O. Box 811, Wenatchee WA 98801 / 509-674-4411.

Columbia Basin Habitat Management Area

BOR Region: Pacific Northwest. See also Desert Wildlife Recreation Area and Potholes Reservoir. Recreation is administered by the State of Washington. Located in central Washington south of Ephrata. The area consists of several small reservoirs and other water features scattered between the communities of Quincy and Othello. Good access is provided from SH 17 and I-90. Fishing areas include Canal, Heart, Windmill, Virgin, Susan, Clark, Goose, Linda, Lyle, Mesa, Warden, and Worth Lakes.

Recreation Contact: Washington Department of Wildlife, 6653 K NE, Moses Lake WA 98837 / 509-765-6641.

Columbia National Wildlife Refuge

BOR Region: Pacific Northwest. See also Columbia Basin Habitat Management Area and Potholes Reservoir. Recreation is administered by the U.S. Fish and Wildlife Service. Located in central Washington near Othello. Access to the area is available from SH 26, SH 262, SH 17, and McManomon Road north out of Othello.

Recreation Contact: U.S. Fish and Wildlife Service, Columbia NWR, 753 E Main, P.O. Drawer F, Othello WA 99344 / 509-488-2668.

Conconully Lake

BOR Region: Pacific Northwest. Recreation is administered by the State of Washington. Located in northern Washington near the community of Conconully. From Omak off SH 215 travel north on Conconully Road to the lake. From Riverside off US 97 travel west on Riverside Cutoff Road to Conconully Road and follow north to the lake.

Recreation Contact: Washington State Parks, Conconully State Park, 2201 N Duncan Dr., Wenatchee WA 98801 / 509-662-0420.

Desert Wildlife Recreation Area

BOR Region: Pacific Northwest. See also Columbia Basin Habitat Management Area. Recreation is administered by the State of Washington. Located in central Washington about 20 miles west of the community of Moses Lake off I-90. Fishing areas include Winchester Reservoir, Winchester Wasteway, Frenchman Hills Wasteway, and numerous small ponds and marshes.

Recreation Contact: Washington Department of Wildlife, 1540 Alder St. NW, Ephrata WA 98823 / 509-754-4624.

Easton Diversion Dam

BOR Region: Pacific Northwest. See also Cle Elum, Kachess, and Keechelus Lakes. Recreation is administered by the State of Washington. Located in central Washington near the town of Easton. Access to the lake is off I-90.

Recreation Contact: Washington State Parks, Lake Easton State Park, 2201 N. Duncan Dr., Wenatchee WA 98801 / 509-662-0420.

Franklin D Roosevelt Lake / Coulee Dam NRA

BOR Region: Pacific Northwest. Recreation is administered by the National Park Service, Colville Confederated Tribes, and Spokane Tribe of Indians. Located in northeastern Washington near the communities of Rice, Gifford, Hunters, Fruitland, Miles, and Lincoln. Several access points are available along SH 21, SH 25 and other minor roads.

Recreation Contact: National Park Service, Coulee Dam NRA, 1008 Crest Dr., Coulee Dam WA 99116 / 509-446-9441. Colville Confederated Tribes, P.O. Box 150, Nespelem WA 99155. Spokane Tribe of Indians, P.O. Box 100, Wellpinit WA 99116.

Kachess Lake

BOR Region: Pacific Northwest. See also Cle Elum and Keechelus Lakes. Recreation is administered by the U.S. Forest Service. Located off I-90 in central Washington, west of Easton.

Recreation Contact: Wenatchee National Forest, P.O. Box 811, Wenatchee WA 98801 / 509-674-4411.

Keechelus Lake

BOR Region: Pacific Northwest. See also Easton Diversion Dam and Kachess Lale. Recreation is administered by the U.S. Forest Service.

Located along I-90, about 15 miles west of Easton, in central Washington, just south of the town of Hyak.

Recreation Contact: Wenatchee National Forest, P.O. Box 811, Wenatchee WA 98801 / 509-674-4411.

Potholes Reservoir

BOR Region: Pacific Northwest. See also Columbia Basin Habitat Management Area and Columbia NWR. Recreation is administered by the State of Washington. Located in central Washington about 15 miles south of the community of Moses Lake. The lake can be accessed from SH 262 off SH 17.

Recreation Contact: Washington Department of Wildlife, 1540 Alder St. NW, Ephrata WA 98823 / 509-754-4624. Washington State Parks, Potholes State Park, 2201 N Duncan Dr., Wenatchee WA 98801 / 509-662-0420.

Quincy Lakes

BOR Region: Pacific Northwest. Recreation is administered by the State of Washington. Quincy Lakes are located in central Washington near the community of George. The lakes can be reached from I-90 near George by following SH 281 north 2 miles, then access roads heading west. These impoundments include Evergreen Reservoir and Burke, Quincy, Babcock Ridge, and Stand Coffin Lakes.

Recreation Contact: Washington Department of Wildlife, 1540 Alder St. NW, Ephrata WA 98823 / 509-754-4624.

Rimrock and Clear Lakes

BOR Region: Pacific Northwest. Recreation is administered by the U.S. Forest Service. Located in south-central Washington south of US 12, about 40 miles west of Yakima in the Cascades.

Recreation Contact: Snoqualmie National Forest, North Bend Ranger District, 42404 SE North Bend Way, North Bend WA 98045 / 425-888-1421.

Roza Diversion Dam

BOR Region: Pacific Northwest. Recreation is administered by the Bureau of Reclamation. Located in central Washington between Yakima and Ellensburg on the Yakima River. The dam can be reached by following SH 821 south from Ellensburg or north out of Yakima.

Recreation Contact: Bureau of Reclamation, 1917 Marsh Rd., Yakima WA 98907 / 509-575-5848.

Scooteney Reservoir

BOR Region: Pacific Northwest. Recreation is administered by the Bureau of Reclamation. Located in southeastern Washington, north of Kennewick. The reservoir can be reached from US 395 near Mesa by traveling north on SH 17. From Othello, follow SH 17 south.

Recreation Contact: Bureau of Reclamation, 800 Scootney Park Rd., Connell WA 99326 / 509-234-0527.

Spectacle Lake

BOR Region: Pacific Northwest. Recreation is administered by the Bureau of Reclamation and State of Washington. Located in northern Washington about 15 miles northwest of Tonasket, near Loomis. The lake can be reached from Tonasket on US 97 by following the Janis-Oroville Westside Road north to Loomis Oroville Road. Travel west about 7 miles on Loomis Oroville Road to the lake.

Recreation Contact: Washington Department of Wildlife, 1540 Alder St. NW, Ephrata WA 98823 / 509-754-4624. Bureau of Reclamation, 32 C St. NW, P.O. Box 815, Ephrata WA 98823 / 509-754-0267.

Primary Game Fish

	BASS	BLUEGILL	CATFISH	CRAPPIE	PIKE	PERCH	SALMON	TROUT	WALLEYE
1 Banks Lake	•		•	•		•	•	•	•
2 Billy Clapp Lake				•		•		•	•
3 Bumping Lake							•	•	
4 Cle Elum Lake							•	•	
5 Columbia Basin HMA	•	•		•		•		•	
6 Columbia NWR	•	•		•		•		•	
7 Conconully Lake	•							•	
8 Desert Wildlife Rec. Area	•			•		•		•	
9 Easton Diversion Dam								•	
10 Franklin D Roosevelt Lake	•			•		•	•	•	•
11 Kachess Lake							•	•	
12 Keechelus Lake							•	•	
13 Potholes Reservoir	•			•		•		•	•
14 Quincy Lakes	•			•		•		•	
15 Rimrock and Clear Lakes							•	•	
16 Roza Diversion Dam							•	•	
17 Scooteney Reservoir	•			•		•			
18 Spectacle Lake								•	

WYOMING

1 Alcova Reservoir
2 Big Sandy Reservoir
3 Bighorn Canyon NRA
4 Boysen Reservoir
5 Buffalo Bill Reservoir
6 Deaver Reservoir
7 Flaming Gorge NRA
8 Fontenelle Reservoir
9 Glendo Reservoir
10 Guernsey Reservoir
11 Jackson Lake
12 Keyhole Reservoir

13 Kortes Reservoir,
    Miracle Mile Area
14 Lake Cameahwait
15 Meeks Cabin Reservoir
16 Newton Lakes
17 Ocean Lake
18 Palisades Reservoir
19 Pathfinder Reservoir
20 Pilot Butte Reservoir
21 Seminoe Reservoir
22 Stateline Reservoir

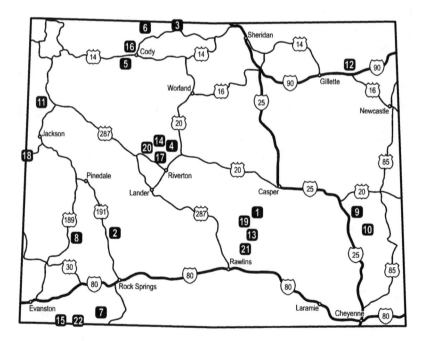

Activities and Facilities

	1	2	3	4	5	6	7	8	9	10	11
1	•	•	•	•	•	•	•	•	•	•	•
2	•	•	•	•	•	•	•		•		•
3	•	•	•					•	•		
4	•	•	•	•	•	•	•	•	•		•
5	•	•	•	•	•	•	•		•		•
6	•	•	•	•				•	•		
7	•	•	•	•	•	•	•	•	•	•	•
8	•	•	•	•	•		•		•		•
9	•	•	•	•	•	•	•	•	•	•	
10	•	•	•	•	•	•	•	•	•	•	
11	•	•	•		•	•	•	•	•	•	
12	•	•	•	•	•	•	•	•	•	•	
13	•	•		•	•		•		•		•
14	•	•	•	•	•	•	•		•		•
15	•	•	•	•	•	•	•		•		
16		•	•	•		•	•		•		•
17	•	•	•	•	•	•	•		•		•
18	•	•	•		•	•	•		•		
19	•	•	•	•	•	•	•	•	•	•	

Alcova Reservoir

BOR Region: Great Plains. See also Kortes and Pathfinder Reservoirs. Recreation is administered by Natrona County. Located in central Wyoming, southwest of Casper, near the town of Alcova. The northern shore of the lake is accessed from SH 220 via CR 406. The southern shore is reached from CR 407 heading south off SH 220.

Recreation Contact: Natrona County Roads, Bridges, and Parks Dept., 538 S Wyoming Blvd., Mills WY 82644 / 307-235-9325.

Big Sandy Reservoir

BOR Region: Upper Colorado. Recreation is administered by the State of Wyoming. Located in southwestern Wyoming about 50 miles north of Rock Springs. The lake can be accessed from Farson by following US 191 north 10 miles to Big Sandy Reservoir Road. Travel east 2 miles to the reservoir.

Recreation Contact: Wyoming State Parks, Big Sandy SRA, 122 W 25th St., Cheyenne WY 82002 / 307-777-6323.

Bighorn Canyon National Recreation Area

BOR Region: Great Plains. Recreation is administered by the National Park Service. Located in southern Montana and northern Wyoming, west of I-90. In Wyoming the area is accessed off US Alt 14 near Lovell. In Montana several secondary state highways, including 313 and 463, lead to the recreation area.

Recreation Contact: National Park Service, Bighorn Canyon NRA, Box 7458, Fort Smith MT 59035 / 406-666-2412.

Boysen Reservoir

BOR Region: Great Plains. See also Lake Cameahwait. Recreation is administered by the State of Wyoming. Located in central Wyoming, north of Riverton. The reservoir can be reached from US 20 or US 26 near the town of Shoshoni.

Recreation Contact: Boysen State Park, Boysen Rt., Shoshoni WY 82649 / 307-876-2769.

Buffalo Bill Reservoir

BOR Region: Great Plains. See also Newton Lakes. Recreation is administered by the State of Wyoming. Located in northwestern Wyoming, east of Yellowstone National Park. The reservoir is 8 miles west of Cody on US 14/16/20 (Yellowstone Highway).

Recreation Contact: Buffalo Bill State Park, 47 Lakeside Rd., Cody WY 82414 / 307-587-9227.

Deaver Reservoir

BOR Region: Great Plains. Recreation is administered by the State of Wyoming. Located in northern Wyoming near the Montana border. The reservoir lies west of US 310 near Deaver. Access roads off SH 114 head north to the reservoir.

Recreation Contact: Wyoming Game and Fish Dept., 2820 State 120, Cody WY 82414 / 307-527-7125.

Flaming Gorge NRA

BOR Region: Upper Colorado. Recreation is administered by the U.S. Forest Service. Located in northeastern Utah and southwestern Wyoming. From Vernal, Utah follow US 191 north 20 miles. Access is provided along US 191 and SH 44 in Utah, and US 191 and SH 530 in Wyoming.

Recreation Contact: Ashley National Forest, Flaming Gorge NRA, P.O. Box 279, Manila UT 84046 / 435-784-3445.

Fontenelle Reservoir

BOR Region: Upper Colorado. Recreation is administered by the Bureau of Land Management. Located in southwestern Wyoming 30 miles northeast of Kemmerer. The reservoir can be accessed from US 189 and SH 372.

Recreation Contact: Bureau of Land Management, Rock Springs District Office, 280 US 191, Rock Springs WY 82901 / 307-352-0256.

Glendo Reservoir

BOR Region: Great Plains. See also Guernsey Reservoir. Recreation is administered by the State of Wyoming. Located in eastern Wyoming about 35 miles southeast of Douglas, near the town of Glendo. From I-25 follow CR 17 (Glendo Park Road) east to the reservoir.

Recreation Contact: Glendo State Park, P.O. Box 398, Glendo WY 82213 / 307-735-4433.

Guernsey Reservoir

BOR Region: Great Plains. See also Glendo Reservoir. Recreation is administered by the State of Wyoming. Located in eastern Wyoming, northeast of Wheatland, 2 miles northwest of the town of Guernsey. The reservoir can be reached from US 26 by following SH 317 north.

Recreation Contact: Guernsey State Park, P.O. Box 429, Guernsey WY 82214 / 307-836-2334.

Jackson Lake

BOR Region: Pacific Northwest. Recreation is administered by the National Park Service. Located in Grand Teton NP, 30 miles north of Jackson. Good access to the lake from US 89, US 191 and US 287.

Recreation Contact: National Park Service, P.O. Drawer 170, Moose WY 83012 / 307-739-3300.

Keyhole Reservoir

BOR Region: Great Plains. Recreation is administered by the State of Wyoming. Located in northeastern Wyoming, east of Gillette, near Moorcroft. From I-90 Exit 165, travel 8 miles north to the reservoir.

Recreation Contact: Keyhole State Park, 353 McKean Rd., Moorcroft WY 82721 / 307-756-3596.

Kortes Reservoir / Miracle Mile Area

BOR Region: Great Plains. See also Alcova and Pathfinder Reservoirs. Recreation is administered by the Bureau of Reclamation. Located on the North Platte River 54 miles southwest of Casper and 34 miles northeast of Rawlins. Access from I-80 via Carbon County Road 351. Northern access from SH 220 via Natrona County Road 407. The Miracle Mile Area extends downstream approximately 5.5 miles from the bottom of Kortes Dam to the boundary of the southern management unit of the Pathfinder National Wildlife Refuge.

Recreation Contact: Bureau of Reclamation, Wyoming Area Office, P.O. Box 1630, Mills WY 82644 / 307-261-5628.

Lake Cameahwait

BOR Region: Great Plains. See also Boysen Reservoir and Ocean

Lake. Recreation is administered by the State of Wyoming. Lake Cameahwait lies west of Boysen Reservoir in central Wyoming. To reach the lake from Shoshoni, follow US 26 west about 6 miles to West Shore Drive. Follow West Shore Drive north to the lake, which is north of the Muddy Creek arm of Boysen Reservoir.

Recreation Contact: Wyoming Game and Fish Department, 2055 Missouri Valley Rd., Pavillion WY 82523 / 307-856-3007.

Meeks Cabin Reservoir

BOR Region: Upper Colorado. See also Stateline Reservoir. Recreation is administered by the U.S. Forest Service. Located in northern Utah and southwest Wyoming. The lake is reached from Mountain View, Wyoming by traveling south on SH 410 for 13 miles to CR 271. Follow CR 271 south for 15 miles to the reservoir.

Recreation Contact: Wasatch-Cache National Forest, Evanston Ranger District, 1565 Hwy 150 S., P.O. Box 1880, Evanston WY 82930 / 307-789-3194.

Newton Lakes

BOR Region: Great Plains. See also Buffalo Bill Reservoir. Recreation is administered by the State of Wyoming. Located in northwestern Wyoming, east of Yellowstone National Park. The lakes are 5 miles northwest of Cody and can be reached by following CR 7 west from SH 120.

Recreation Contact: Wyoming Game and Fish Dept., 2820 State 120, Cody WY 82414 / 307-527-7125.

Ocean Lake

BOR Region: Great Plains. See also Lake Cameahwait and Pilot Butte Reservoir. Recreation is administered by the State of Wyoming. Located in central Wyoming about 20 miles west of Riverton. The lake is north of US 26 near the town of Kinnear.

Recreation Contact: Wyoming Game and Fish Department, 2055 Missouri Valley Rd., Pavillion WY 82523 / 307-856-3007.

Palisades Reservoir

BOR Region: Pacific Northwest. Recreation is administered by the

U.S. Forest Service. Located in eastern Idaho and western Wyoming, east of Idaho Falls near Alpine, Wyoming. Access is available along US 26, south of Palisades, Idaho.

Recreation Contact: Targhee National Forest, 420 Bridge St., Saint Anthony ID 83445 / 208-624-3151.

Pathfinder Reservoir

BOR Region: Great Plains. See also Alcova, Kortes, and Seminoe Reservoirs. Recreation is administered by the Bureau of Land Management and Natrona County. Located in central Wyoming about 45 miles southwest of Casper. From Casper, follow SH 220 south about 36 miles to CR 409 (Pathfinder Road). Follow CR 409 south to the reservoir.

Recreation Contact: Bureau of Land Management, Rawlins District Office, 1300 N 3rd St., Rawlins WY 82301 / 307-324-7171. Natrona County Roads, Bridges, and Parks Dept., 538 S Wyoming Blvd., Mills WY 82644 / 307-235-9325.

Pilot Butte Reservoir

BOR Region: Great Plains. See also Ocean Lake. Recreation is administered by the State of Wyoming. Located in central Wyoming, 25 miles west of Riverton, on US 26 near Morton.

Recreation Contact: Wyoming Game and Fish Dept., 2055 Missouri Valley Rd., Pavillion WY 82523 / 307-856-3007.

Seminoe Reservoir

BOR Region: Great Plains. See also Pathfinder Reservoir. Recreation is administered by the State of Wyoming. Located in south-central Wyoming, northeast of Rawlins, 38 miles north of Sinclair. Access from I-80 is via Carbon County Road 351 north (Seminoe Road).

Recreation Contact: Seminoe State Park, Seminoe Dam Rt., Sinclair WY 82334 / 307-320-3013.

Stateline Reservoir

BOR Region: Upper Colorado. See also Meeks Cabin Reservoir. Recreation is administered by the U.S. Forest Service. Located in northern Utah and southwest Wyoming about 20 miles south of Mountain View, Wyoming. Follow SH 410 south for about 7 miles from Mountain View.

Follow CR 246 south for 8 miles to the national forest boundary and then south on FSR 72 for 5 miles. Forest Service Road 72 is an improved gravel road.

Recreation Contact: Wasatch-Cache National Forest, Mountain View Ranger District, P.O. Box 129, Mountain View WY 82939 / 307-782-6555.

Primary Game Fish

	BASS	BLUEGILL	CATFISH	CRAPPIE	PIKE	PERCH	SALMON	TROUT	WALLEYE
1 Alcova Reservoir								•	•
2 Big Sandy Reservoir			•					•	
3 Bighorn Canyon NRA								•	•
4 Boysen Reservoir							•		•
5 Buffalo Bill Reservoir								•	
6 Deaver Reservoir			•					•	•
7 Flaming Gorge NRA	•						•	•	
8 Fontenelle Reservoir								•	
9 Glendo Reservoir			•			•		•	•
10 Guernsey Reservoir			•			•			•
11 Jackson Lake								•	
12 Keyhole Reservoir	•				•				•
13 Kortes Reservoir								•	•
14 Lake Cameahwait	•	•		•		•			
15 Meeks Cabin Reservoir								•	
16 Newton Lakes								•	
17 Ocean Lake		•		•		•		•	•
18 Palisades Reservoir							•	•	
19 Pathfinder Reservoir								•	•
20 Pilot Butte Reservoir			•					•	
21 Seminoe Reservoir								•	•
22 Stateline Reservoir								•	

Appendix A

Bureau of Reclamation Regions

Bureau of Reclamation Headquarters
1849 C St. NW
Washington, DC 20240 .... *Phone:* 202-208-3484

Great Plains Regional Office
P.O. Box 36900
Billings, MT 59107 .... *Phone:* 406-247-7600

Lower Colorado Regional Office
P.O. Box 61470
Boulder City, NV 89006 .... *Phone:* 702-293-8411

Mid-Pacific Regional Office
Federal Office Building
2800 Cottage Way
Sacramento, CA 95825 .... *Phone:* 916-978-5000

Pacific Northwest Regional Office
1150 N Curtis Rd., Suite 100
Boise, ID 83706 .... *Phone:* 208-378-5012

Upper Colorado Regional Office
125 S State St., Room 6107
Salt Lake City, UT 84138 .... *Phone:* 801-524-3600

APPENDIX B

Alphabetical List of Lakes

Lakes	*Page*
Agate Reservoir	80
Alcova Reservoir	111
Altus Lake	77
American Falls Reservoir	45
Anderson Ranch Reservoir	46
Angostura Reservoir	88
Apache Lake	8
Arbuckle Lake	77
Arrowrock Reservoir	46
Avalon Reservoir	69
Banks Lake	103
Bartlett Reservoir	9
Belle Fourche Reservoir	88
Beulah Reservoir	81
Big Sandy Reservoir	112
Bighorn Canyon National Recreation Area	56
Billy Clapp Lake	104
Black Canyon Reservoir	46
Blue Mesa Reservoir	31
Boca Reservoir	17
Bonham Reservoir	31
Bonny Reservoir	32
Box Butte Reservoir	61
Boysen Reservoir	112
Brantley Reservoir	69
Brekken-Holmes Recreation Area	74
Buffalo Bill Reservoir	112
Bully Creek Reservoir	81
Bumping Lake	104
Caballo Reservoir	70
Cachuma Lake	17
Calamus Reservoir	61

Lakes	**Page**
Canyon Ferry Lake	56
Canyon Lake	9
Carter Lake	32
Cascade Reservoir	46
Causey Reservoir	94
Cedar Bluff Reservoir	52
Cheney Reservoir	52
Choke Canyon Reservoir	91
Cibola National Wildlife Refuge	9
Clark Canyon Reservoir	56
Cle Elum Lake	104
Clear Lake	81
Cold Springs Reservoir	81
Colorado River Wildlife Area	32
Columbia Basin Habitat Management Area	104
Columbia National Wildlife Refuge	105
Conconully Lake	105
Contra Loma Reservoir	18
Cottonwood #1 Reservoir	32
Crane Prairie Reservoir	81
Crawford Reservoir	33
Crescent Lake	82
Crystal Reservoir	33
Currant Creek Reservoir	95
Davis Creek Reservoir	61
Davis Dam — Lake Mohave	10
Deadwood Reservoir	47
Deaver Reservoir	113
Deer Creek Reservoir	95
Deerfield Reservoir	88
Desert Wildlife Recreation Area	105
Devils Lake	74
East Canyon Reservoir	95
East Park Reservoir	18
East Portal Reservoir	34
Easton Diversion Dam	106
Echo Reservoir	95

Lakes   *Page*

Edward A. Patterson Lake 74
El Vado Reservoir 70
Elephant Butte Reservoir 70
Emigrant Lake 82
Enders Reservoir 61
Flaming Gorge NRA 96
Flatiron Reservoir 34
Folsom Lake 18
Fontenelle Reservoir 113
Fort Cobb Lake 77
Foss Reservoir 77
Franklin D Roosevelt Lake / Coulee Dam NRA 106
Fresno Reservoir 57
Fruitgrowers Reservoir 34
Gerber Reservoir 82
Gibson Reservoir 57
Glendo Reservoir 113
Green Mountain Camp 34
Green Mountain Reservoir 35
Guernsey Reservoir 114
Gunnison River Fishing Easements 35
Harry Strunk Reservoir 61
Havasu National Wildlife Refuge 10
Haystack Reservoir 82
Helena Valley Reservoir 57
Henry Hagg Lake 83
Heron Reservoir 70
Hoover Dam 11
Horseshoe Reservoir 11
Horsethief Canyon State Wildlife Area 35
Horsetooth Reservoir 35
Howard Prairie Lake 83
Hugh Butler Reservoir 62
Hungry Horse Reservoir 57
Huntington North Reservoir 96
Hyatt Reservoir 83
Hyrum Reservoir 96

Lakes	*Page*

Imperial National Wildlife Refuge	12
Imperial Reservoir	11
Island Park Reservoir	47
Jackson Gulch Reservoir	36
Jackson Lake	114
Jamestown Reservoir	74
Jenkinson Lake	20
Joes Valley Reservoir	96
Jordanelle Reservoir	97
Kachess Lake	106
Keechelus Lake	106
Keith Sebeluis Reservoir	52
Keswick Reservoir	20
Keyhole Reservoir	114
Kirwin National Wildlife Refuge	52
Kortes Reservoir / Miracle Mile Area	114
Lahontan Reservoir	66
Lake Berryessa	20
Lake Byron	88
Lake Cahuilla	21
Lake Cameahwait	114
Lake Casitas	21
Lake Elwell	58
Lake Estes	36
Lake Granby	36
Lake Havasu	10
Lake Lowell	47
Lake Mead National Recreation Area	12
Lake Meredith National Recreation Area	91
Lake Minatare State Recreation Area	62
Lake Pleasant	12
Lake Powell — Glen Canyon NRA	13
Lake Solano	21
Lake Sumner	71
Lake Tahoe	21
Lake Texana	91
Lake Thunderbird	77

Lakes	*Page*
Lake Tschida	75
Lake Waha	47
Lake Walcott	48
Lake Woollomes	22
Leasburg Diversion Dam	71
Lemon Reservoir	36
Lewiston Lake	22
Little Panoche Dam	22
Little Wood River Reservoir	48
Los Banos Reservoir	23
Lost Creek Reservoir	97
Lovewell Reservoir	53
Mann Creek Reservoir	48
Mann Lake Reservoir A	49
Marys Lake	37
McGee Creek Reservoir	78
McKay Reservoir	83
McPhee Reservoir	37
Meeks Cabin Reservoir	97
Merritt Reservoir	62
Millerton Lake	23
Mittry Lake Wildlife Area	13
Montour Wildlife / Recreation Management Area	49
Moon Lake Reservoir	98
Morrow Point Reservoir	37
Nambe Falls Reservoir	71
Navajo Reservoir	38
Nelson Reservoir	58
New Melones Lake	23
Newton Lakes	115
Newton Reservoir	98
Ocean Lake	115
Ochoco Reservoir	84
Owyhee Reservoir	84
Pactola Reservoir	89
Palisades Reservoir	49
Paonia Reservoir	38

Lakes	*Page*
Pathfinder Reservoir	116
Phillips Lake	84
Pilot Butte Reservoir	116
Pineview Reservoir	98
Pinewood Lake	38
Pishkun Reservoir	58
Platoro Reservoir	38
Potholes Reservoir	107
Prineville Reservoir	84
Prosser Creek Reservoir	24
Pueblo Reservoir	39
Quincy Lakes	107
Red Fleet Reservoir	98
Ridgway Reservoir	39
Rifle Gap Reservoir	39
Rimrock and Clear Lakes	107
Ririe Reservoir	49
Rockport Reservoir	99
Roza Diversion Dam	108
Ruedi Reservoir	39
Rye Patch Reservoir	67
Saguaro Lake	13
Salton Sea SRA and NWR	24
San Justo Reservoir	24
San Luis Reservoir	24
Scofield Reservoir	99
Scooteney Reservoir	108
Seminoe Reservoir	116
Shadehill Reservoir	89
Shadow Mountain Lake	40
Shasta Lake	25
Sherman Reservoir	62
Silver Jack Reservoir	40
Soldiers Meadow Reservoir	50
Spectacle Lake	108
Squaw Leap Management Area	25
Stampede Reservoir	25

Lakes	*Page*
Starvation Reservoir	99
Stateline Reservoir	99
Steinaker Reservoir	100
Stony Gorge Reservoir	25
Strawberry Reservoir	100
Sugar Pine Reservoir	26
Swanson Reservoir	63
Taylor Park Reservoir	40
Taylor River State Wildlife Area	40
Theodore Roosevelt Lake	13
Thief Valley Reservoir	85
Tom Steed Lake	78
Trinity Lake	26
Turquoise Lake	41
Twin Buttes Reservoir	92
Twin Lakes Reservoir	41
Unity Reservoir	85
Upper Stillwater Reservoir	100
Vallecito Reservoir	41
Vega Reservoir	42
Waconda Reservoir	53
Warm Springs Reservoir	85
Webster Reservoir	53
Whiskeytown Lake	26
Wickiup Reservoir	85
Willard Reservoir	100
Willow Creek Reservoir (Colorado)	42
Willow Creek Reservoir (Montana)	59
Winters Creek Lake	63
Woodston Diversion Dam	53

New Release!

The Perfect Companion to
Bureau of Reclamation Lakes Guide...

Lakeside Recreation

Corps of Engineers Volume I
Western United States

The most comprehensive guide available on
the Corps of Egineers projects!

Find the ideal setting for outdoor recreation in this definitive guide to the Corps of Engineers lakes and reservoirs!

Lakeside Recreation

Corps of Engineers Volume I
Western United States

Lakeside Recreation describes 148 lakes and reservoirs constructed by the US Army Corps of Engineers in the Western United States. You'll find detailed information on over 1,200 lakeside parks and recreational facilities surrounding these water areas. These Corps projects include over 800 campgrounds offering more than 35,000 campsites. *Lakeside Recreation* is the most complete and up-to-date book available on the Corps lakes.

The 280-page book includes a map of each lake showing the location of all recreation areas. Detailed descriptions inform you of the many recreational opportunities available. Specific information for the angler includes types of fish and location of boat ramps, fishing piers and marinas.

Each lake description includes a chart with information on the number of campsites available at each recreation area and the number of hookups for the RVer. The chart also depicts other facilities in each park area such as restrooms, showers, drinking water, trails, marinas, boat ramps, dump stations, picnic facilities, swimming beaches, and amphitheaters.

The lakes offer everything from highly developed, modern facilities to quiet, secluded spots to simply escape for a while. There are areas to park your home on wheels and areas that can only be reached by hiking or boating. Some lakes offer majestic scenic views of deep river canyons while others unfold along the great open plains. If you like camping under the stars, playing in the outdoors, or making waves in the water, there's a lake just waiting for you!

Use the order form on the next page or call 800-455-2207

Order Form — Lakeside Recreation

Phone: 800-455-2207

Fax: 913-541-0636

Mail: Roundabout Publications
P.O. Box 19235
Lenexa, KS 66285

Yes, please send me the new book *Lakeside Recreation: Corps of Engineers Volume I • Western United States* (Item # 4010). If I am not completely satisfied with my order, I may return it within 90 days for a full refund.

Item #	**4010**
Qty.	
Each	$14.95
Subtotal	
S&H	3.00
Tax	
Total	

Shipping & Handling:

$3.00 any size order

Kansas Residents:

Add 4.9% sales tax

Payment Method:

❑ Check or Money Order ❑ Visa ❑ MasterCard

Name _____

Address _____

City, State, Zip _____

Credit Card # _____

Exp. Date_____ Phone _____

Signature _____